THE EFFECTIVE EXECUTIVE EDUCATION ADVISOR

From Manager to Visionary Leader

Eric Greenberg

Copyright © 2023 Eric Greenberg.

All rights reserved.

No part of this publication may be reproduced, distributed, or transmitted in any form or by any means, including photocopying, recording, or other electronic or mechanical methods, without the prior written permission of the publisher, except as permitted by U.S. copyright law. For permission requests, contact the author.

THE EFFECTIVE EXECUTIVE EDUCATION ADVISOR
From Manager to Visionary Leader

Cover design - Eric Greenberg

Table Of Contents

Introduction to the World of Executive Education 1
    Taylorism and Fordism 2
    The G.I. Bill 4
    The Role of Universities 6
    The Need for Continuing Education 6
  The Benefits of University Advisory Boards 8
    Individual Benefits 9
    Connections and Partnerships 10
    Looking Ahead 11
Assessing Advisory Board Openings and Opportunities 12
    Online Resources and Job Platforms 14
    Personal Outreach and Building Relationships 15
  Working on a Corporate Advisory Board 16
    Key Responsibilities 17
    Meetings and Discussions 18
    Personal Networking 19
    Conducting Ongoing Research 19
    Looking Ahead 20
Leveraging Your Industry Experience and Insights 22
    Understanding Obstacles and Risks in Context 23
  Case Studies and Lessons Learned 27
    Amazon's Monitron System 29
    Ryder's Customer Advisory Board Program 31

- Adobe's Customer Advisory Board Program 31
- Curriculum Design and Program Content 32
  - Curriculum Development and Program Design 34
  - Industry Knowledge and Subject Matter Experts 37
  - Looking Ahead 38
- Advocating for Diversity, Equity, and Inclusion 39
  - Creating a Legacy of Diversity, Equity, and Inclusion 41
  - Ongoing Support for Program Graduates 42
  - Inclusive Recruitment and Selection Practices 43
    - Establishing a Diverse Talent Pipeline 44
    - Inclusive Selection and Admissions Processes 44
    - Diversity Among Instructors and Staff 48
    - Conducting Research and Updating Perspectives 49
  - Ensuring an Inclusive and Equitable Learning Environment 50
    - Different Teaching Styles 50
    - Removing Barriers to Accessibility 51
    - Creating an Inclusive Culture 53
    - Looking Ahead 54
- Collaborations Between Academia and Industry 55
  - Customized Educational Solutions 57
  - Applied Research and Models of Innovation 58
  - Establishing Roles and Responsibilities in Joint Ventures 60
  - Promoting an Inclusive Culture 61
- Cross-Disciplinary Initiatives 62
  - Creating Effective Teams 64
  - Looking Ahead 66

- Program Growth and Sustainability 67
  - Maximizing Your Personal Branding 69
  - Building Interest Among Prospective Students 70
  - Financial Stability and Resource Management 75
  - Diversifying Revenue Streams 77
  - Looking Ahead 82
- Continuous Improvement and Evaluating Program Success 83
  - Highlighting the Impact of Continuous Improvement 85
  - Program Evaluations 86
  - Program Impact on Participants and Organizations 88
  - Needs Assessments and Student Satisfaction 90
  - Program Goals and Learning Objectives 91
  - Efficiency and Wasted Effort 91
  - Relevance of Program Topics 92
  - Improvement and Innovation 94
  - Types of Innovation 95
  - Incorporating Outside Perspectives 96
  - Communicating Value 97
  - Looking Ahead 98
- Balancing Multiple Leadership Roles 99
  - Time Management and Prioritization 101
  - Conflicts of Interest 105
  - Being an Effective and Inspiring Board Member 106

List Of Figures

Figure 1: Even though competing companies had work that was more interesting, Ford factories offered better compensation and benefits. 4

Figure 2: The immediate post-war period required millions of people to rapidly adjust both in the workforce and their personal lives. 5

Figure 3: Executive education helps leaders balance a range of business priorities, social changes, and market influences...7

Figure 4: Advisory board members often belong to different groups and industries. 8

Figure 5: The university itself and advisory board members both derive benefits from the relationship..9

Figure 6: When assessing advisory board opportunities, ask detailed questions to ensure you fully understand the role. 13

Figure 7: LinkedIn connects individuals, companies, and schools via a centralized platform... 14

Figure 8: Corporate advisory board members handle a variety of administrative, technical, and strategic tasks.. 17

Figure 9: Proposed federal rulings must take into account comments and opinions from the public and industry. 20

Figure 10: National-level influences and regulations are highly complex and difficult to manage even for global entities. 25

Figure 11: The Sugar Technology Institute is an example of an effective collaborative arrangement between organizations in different sectors. 27

Figure 12: Your organizational capabilities in a particular functional area won't always align with other companies' strengths and weaknesses. Consider the impact of these differences as you assess potential learnings from case studies... 28

Figure 13: David Kolb's four-stage approach is one theory of learning among many... 33

Figure 14: Open-ended questions like those used in the Start-Stop-Continue method encourage students to provide details and explain their thoughts about the program... 36

Figure 15: Individuals have inherent traits as well as variable characteristics that may change based on their circumstances or choices. 40

Figure 16: Creating an inclusive application process requires a multi-pronged approach that addresses the potential for bias and improves accessibility. 43

Figure 17: Gender and racial diversity among full-time faculty is still severely lacking. 48

Figure 18: Various teaching strategies have different focus areas and levels of student participation. 51

Figure 19: Alt text should be descriptive enough to fully explain the purpose and content of an image. 52

Figure 20: Each entity in a collaboration contributes different elements to the whole. 56

Figure 21: Multiple companies and nonprofit organizations may periodically collaborate on joint initiatives. 58

Figure 22: Academia and industry have fundamentally different purposes that can cause friction during collaborative projects. 59

Figure 23: In a cross-functional model, team members often have different approaches, methods, and viewpoints. 64

Figure 24: When building cross-functional teams, it's prudent to establish common methods and standardized processes as early as possible. 65

Figure 25: Marketing materials should showcase the major strengths of your program and appeal specifically to your target audience. 68

Figure 26: The value of social media lies in how much it compounds your reach and allows you to access not only your own network but also those of your contacts. 69

Figure 27: A sample budget helps people who are interested in your program understand the financial side of enrollment. 73

Figure 28: Expenses may relate to multiple different functional areas such as marketing and software. 75

Figure 29: Exploring several revenue streams ensures your program isn't wholly reliant on any single source. 77

Figure 30: Each stage of DMAIC poses a central question about the problem. 84

Figure 31: This method of evaluation considers multiple facets of how students experience the program and relate to the university as a whole. 87

Figure 32: Using multiple sources of quantitative and qualitative data allows you to develop a more thorough understanding of the program. 89

Figure 33: A skills matrix simplifies the process of identifying each person's interests and comparing skill sets in a larger group.................. 93

Figure 34: Product innovation and process innovation are distinct from one another with separate core purposes. 95

Figure 35: Advisory board members must balance their responsibility to the university against their individual priorities and the demands of their organizations.. 100

Figure 36: Tasks mapped on an Eisenhower Matrix can fall into one of four quadrants based on urgency and importance................................ 102

Figure 37: For better visual organization, you can color code tasks in a planner or app to match the Eisenhower Matrix. 103

Figure 38: There are many different conflicts of interest that can stem from personal or professional connections. 105

Figure 39: As you become more comfortable, you'll progressively take a more active role to inspire, mentor, and lead others. 107

1

Introduction to the World of Executive Education

In the modern workforce, training is more than a corporate box to check or a fringe perk for a few individuals. It's evolved into an essential expectation for employees and a critical aspect of career development. LinkedIn's 2018 Workforce Learning Report revealed that 94 percent of employees would be more likely to stay with a company that actively invested in their professional growth.

This concept of continuous learning extends into the executive levels. Executive education combines scientific principles with concepts traditionally associated with business management. From cultivating soft skills like communication to building technical competency, there are plenty of opportunities for leaders to pursue ongoing education in virtually any field.

In addition to creating more well-rounded leaders, executive education can result in a tangible impact to your business. A study conducted by the Association for Talent Development showed that companies with formalized training programs experienced higher profit margins at a rate of 24 percent. Investments in training also yielded improvements in productivity, retention, and employee engagement.

In order to fully understand the importance of executive education, it's first necessary to explore its history and social context. Professional development is closely related to the evolution of management theories. These principles and practices have changed over time to reflect the needs of business leaders at different points throughout history.

Even though continuing education is a major priority in today's business world, the idea of executive education dates back over a century. As organizations came to recognize the value of scientific management and standardized business processes, they also saw the need for training that could expand the skills of their managerial teams. Executive education emerged to meet this demand. Instructional programs provided managers with the tools they needed to analyze internal processes, identify inefficiencies, and implement improvements.

Over time, the field of executive education branched out to encompass leadership skills, strategic thinking, and organizational development. It evolved beyond its original focus on pure operational efficiency. Executive education will likely expand again as society acclimates to modern-day challenges such as remote work and increased automation.

Taylorism and Fordism

Executive education was partially built upon Taylorism, a management theory developed by Frederick Winslow Taylor in the late nineteenth and early twentieth centuries. Taylorism became known as scientific management. Its aim was to improve efficiency by taking a scientific approach to designing workflows and internal processes.

Taylor believed the most effective way to increase productivity was to scientifically analyze each task and determine the most efficient method of performing them. He studied workflows according to time and motion to consider the least taxing techniques. Taylor also devised incentive programs to motivate workers and ensure their full participation.

Henry Ford built upon the tenets of Taylorism by creating his own system of mass production. Fordism specifically addressed the use of assembly lines and standardization in manufacturing. This method revolutionized industrial processes throughout the twentieth century.

Fordism increased factory output and reduced the costs associated with production. This allowed Ford to meet customer demands and scale rapidly without sacrificing efficiency. Although Ford's techniques were designed for use in the automobile industry, they spread to other sectors when companies recognized Ford's success.

The principles of Fordism contributed to economic growth and higher rates of employment. Henry Ford himself was also instrumental in challenging traditional labor norms of the time. In 1914, he instituted an eight-hour working day and increased wages far beyond the average. The desirable schedule and higher pay reduced turnover at Ford plants, which preserved employees' knowledge and experience.

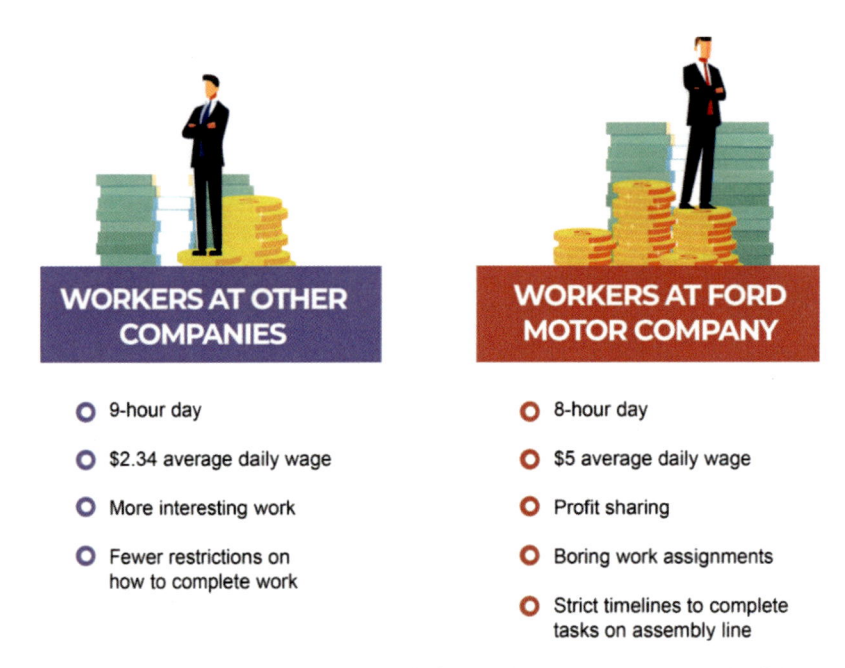

WORKERS AT OTHER COMPANIES	WORKERS AT FORD MOTOR COMPANY
○ 9-hour day	○ 8-hour day
○ $2.34 average daily wage	○ $5 average daily wage
○ More interesting work	○ Profit sharing
○ Fewer restrictions on how to complete work	○ Boring work assignments
	○ Strict timelines to complete tasks on assembly line

Figure 1: Even though competing companies had work that was more interesting, Ford factories offered better compensation and benefits.

The G.I. Bill

The G.I. Bill, also known as the Servicemen's Readjustment Act of 1944, had a profound impact on education after the end of World War II. The bill provided financial assistance for veterans to pursue education and training. It enabled them to acquire different skills than those used in the military, if desired, and opened pathways to train future executives for high-paying positions during the postwar economic boom.

Many universities and business schools began tailoring their programs to meet the needs of veterans. Executive education programs focused on core business concepts such as finance and human resources that veterans would need to transition to civilian life. A lingering question, however, was whether the job market would support the drastic shift from wartime production to peace.

MILITARY WORK ENVIRONMENT

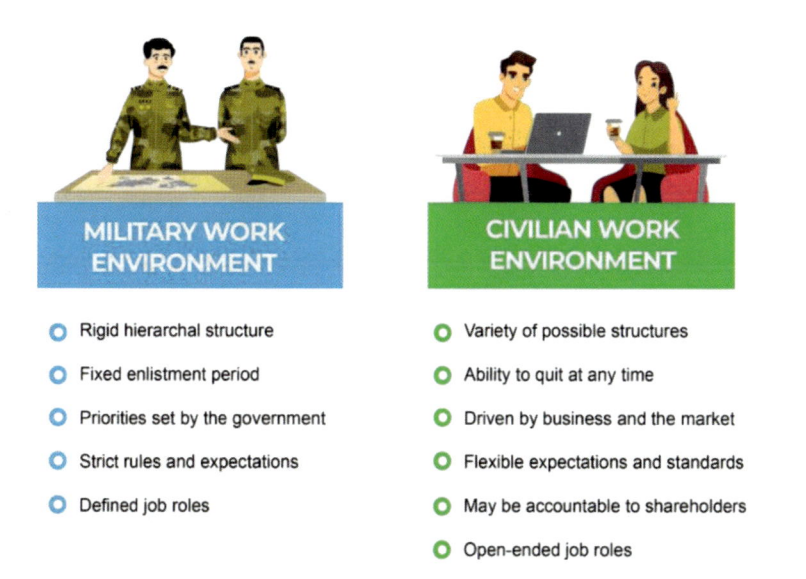

- Rigid hierarchal structure
- Fixed enlistment period
- Priorities set by the government
- Strict rules and expectations
- Defined job roles

CIVILIAN WORK ENVIRONMENT

- Variety of possible structures
- Ability to quit at any time
- Driven by business and the market
- Flexible expectations and standards
- May be accountable to shareholders
- Open-ended job roles

Figure 2: The immediate post-war period required millions of people to rapidly adjust both in the workforce and their personal lives.

During the war, the government urged Americans to be judicious about how they consumed essential items and materials. In addition to rationing, many people saved their money and declined to purchase things like new furniture if they thought it might impede the war effort. Therefore, once the conflict was over, they had both the time and the ability to make those larger purchases.

As a result, many factories and companies that had supported the war effort were able to convert their facilities to manufacture everyday necessities. As these organizations expanded, there were new roles available for fresh leaders. The G.I Bill helped diversify the talent pool for executives and allowed veterans to repurpose the leadership skills they'd first honed in a military setting.

The Role of Universities

Academic institutions have played a crucial role in shaping executive education. Prominent universities such as Harvard and MIT have supported the research of influential professors and experts in the field. For example, Michael E. Porter established himself as a leading authority on economics and business throughout an illustrious career at Harvard Business School.

Porter's work has been used by organizations all over the world. His research on competitive advantage has been instrumental for understanding strategic positioning and decision-making. Harvard Business School is known for its case study method, which encourages executives to analyze real-world business challenges. This approach has been widely adopted in other executive education programs.

Some institutions such as the University of Pennsylvania's Wharton School of Business have taken executive education a step further by offering customized programs. Wharton offers small-group open enrollment with course selections tailored to your organizational needs. Leading companies such as Nissan, Google, and China Minsheng Bank have already partnered with Wharton to develop their own executive education programs.

The Need for Continuing Education

Ongoing training and personal development are crucial in today's dynamic global economy. Advanced technologies such as AI, machine learning, and natural language processing continue to disrupt traditional methods of operation. The rise of new business models requires adaptive leaders who are willing to invest in their own skills and competencies.

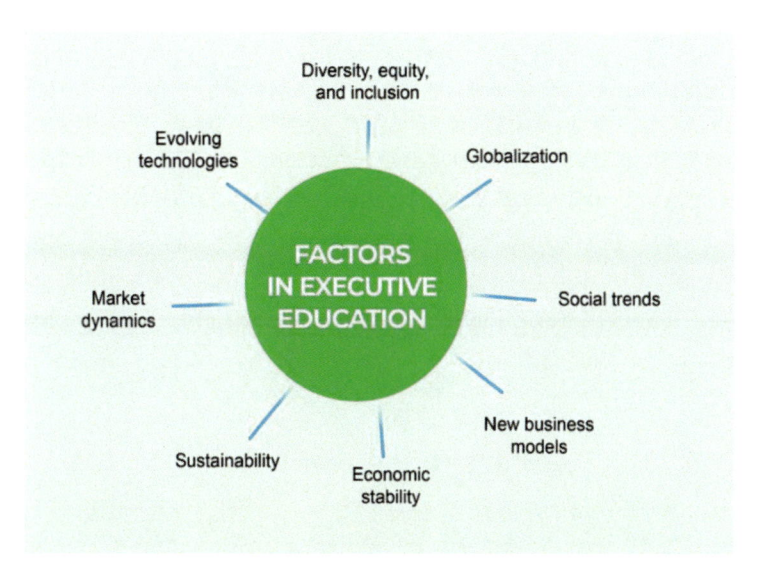

Figure 3: Executive education helps leaders balance a range of business priorities, social changes, and market influences.

As an executive or advisory board member, it's part of your role to define how your organization prepares for the future. This entrepreneurial mindset should extend to your personal growth as well. By engaging in education both as a leader and a student, you're making a commitment to keep an open mind and remain agile in the face of change.

Investing in your own professional development also sets a positive example for others in your organization. If your peers and subordinates see that you're pursuing additional training, they're less likely to feel conflicted about doing the same. In this way, seeking out opportunities to improve your skills contributes toward a culture of continuous learning and discourages complacency.

The Benefits of University Advisory Boards

University advisory boards are composed of stakeholders from different industries, community organizations, and academic specialties. These experts collaborate with the institution to provide guidance and promote innovative, multifaceted approaches to education. Since each member of the board brings a unique perspective, this structure minimizes the likelihood that academic programs will become too narrow in scope.

ADVISORY BOARD PARTICIPANTS

INDUSTRY LEADERS | NONPROFIT ORGANIZATIONS | RESEARCHERS AND ACADEMICS | UNIVERSITY ALUMNI | COMMUNITY GROUPS

Figure 4: Advisory board members often belong to different groups and industries.

Essentially, advisory boards provide a shared space for academia, the business world, and nonprofit groups to collaborate. Board members are often highly experienced in their respective fields. Their backgrounds and achievements enable them to discuss emerging trends, best practices, and potential challenges from a real-world perspective. This type of open dialogue helps universities align their programs with the needs of the job market and keep a pulse on the skill sets that are currently in demand.

After all, a business school that only focuses on hypothetical situations may be out of touch with the latest trends in the market and the workforce. If professors are drawing upon their own experiences from years prior, they won't be able to share firsthand information from the recent past. For instance, a professor who successfully led a company pre-pandemic and AI, wouldn't have direct insights about the impact of automation or how to manage the growing demand for flexible work arrangements.

University advisory boards help bridge this gap by involving contemporary leaders and soliciting their opinions about how to keep coursework current and fresh. Members also serve as points of contact for professors to update their understanding of the market and develop new methods of instruction as needed.

Individual Benefits

If you serve on a university advisory board, you may not be compensated for your time in a traditional sense. However, there are numerous advantages to pursuing these positions that fall beyond financial benefit. Since advisory boards consist of a larger group, they serve as a valuable opportunity to connect with fellow leaders and learn how other organizations operate.

INDIVIDUAL BENEFITS
- Develop critical thinking and problem-solving skills
- Mentorship and networking
- Personal branding opportunities
- Prestige and recognition

UNIVERSITY BENEFITS
- Input from diverse perspectives
- Industry insights from leaders
- Connections and partnerships with businesses
- Staying informed about industry trends

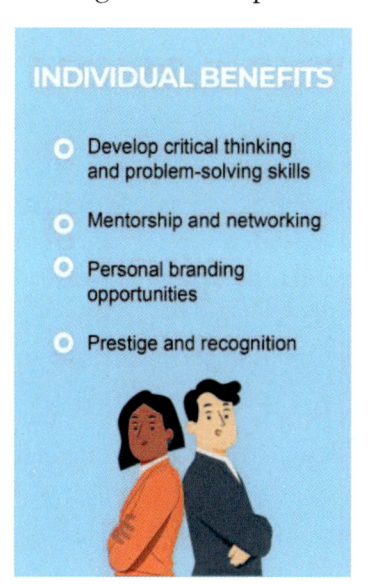

Figure 5: The university itself and advisory board members both derive benefits from the relationship.

These types of collaborative settings foster open discussion and the free exchange of knowledge between leaders in a way that's difficult to accomplish elsewhere. Working alongside individuals from other industries can help you develop your critical thinking or cultivate new strengths like strategic planning.

Joining a university advisory board will also enhance your personal branding and reputation in your field. Serving on a reputable board showcases your dedication to future generations and reinforces your commitment to your profession as a whole. Being associated with an advisory board also establishes you as an authority, which can lead to new opportunities such as speaking engagements or media exposure.

Additionally, advisory boards provide you with a channel to seek out mentorship and personal development from others. If you need guidance on how to advance your career or tackle a specific challenge within your organization, you already have access to several accomplished professionals with a wealth of experience.

Connections and Partnerships

University advisory boards provide a common link to facilitate ongoing relationships with board members' external organizations. Partnerships with industry can yield research opportunities, student funding, internships, and job placements for graduates. Making connections not only provides students with access to industry resources, but it also bolsters university engagement within the local community.

Participating organizations can benefit from these arrangements by leveraging the prestige of being associated with a university and building a mutually beneficial pipeline of talent. For example, an intern who spends a semester at a partner company might later return to pursue a permanent position. Since they've already worked there in the past, there's less ambiguity about whether they'll be successful or the company will be a good fit. This reduces the amount of time, energy, and effort needed to fill the position and secure that individual a place in the workforce.

Furthermore, maintaining an ongoing relationship makes it simpler for companies to offer continuing education programs through an affiliated university. With an established partnership, employees and executives won't need to search for a school if they choose to pursue additional education or training.

Looking Ahead

In this first chapter, we introduced the idea of executive education and reviewed key historical influences such as Taylorism and Fordism. We also discussed the need for continuing education opportunities and how groups like university advisory boards influence executive education programs.

The next chapter will expand upon this foundation by discussing various types of advisory boards and their roles. This will include a section on how to find open board positions and assess whether a particular role is the right fit for your needs.

2

Assessing Advisory Board Openings and Opportunities

If you're interested in joining an advisory board, the first step is assessing which opportunities are the best match for your skills, interests, and personal preferences. It's also important to consider your career aspirations and what you hope to gain by serving on the board. Identifying your priorities in advance will make it easier to find the right role as you begin your search.

A simple way to narrow your list of options is to evaluate the reputation and resources of each institution with an open position. While this shouldn't be the only factor in your selection process, you need to do your due diligence to confirm that a university, foundation, or nonprofit is well respected. This might involve researching its leadership, speaking with representatives, or evaluating the organization's publications.

Analyzing the group's recent accomplishments provides insight into its overall capabilities as well as its standing within the academic, business, or global community. You should also investigate whether the institution has a support system in place for advisors to build their personal brands and cultivate a network with other professionals. If you're evaluating university advisory boards, exploring the school's executive education programs can help you better understand its existing connections and determine which prominent alumni have graduated from its courses.

QUESTIONS TO ASK ABOUT AN ADVISORY BOARD

- What industries or groups do the current members represent?
- What are the roles and responsibilities?
- How long do members serve on the board?
- How many people serve on the board?
- What are some examples of successful interactions between industry and the school?
- When are meetings held, and are they in person or remote?
- What steps does the school take to create a diverse applicant pool?

Figure 6: When assessing advisory board opportunities, ask detailed questions to ensure you fully understand the role.

As you develop a longlist of prospective organizations, make sure you assess the composition of the current board. When in doubt, don't hesitate to request additional information or ask tough questions. Consider the diversity of the board, members' responsibilities, and the proposed term of service. Participating on an advisory board is a major commitment, and you deserve full transparency as you come to a decision.

Online Resources and Job Platforms

In many cases, finding opportunities to serve on an advisory board will require proactive effort on your part. Unless you have an existing relationship with a university, advisory boards won't necessarily contact you about open positions, especially if they have other applicants who have already expressed interest.

Instead of hoping to be approached or attempting to network in person at conferences, you can take charge of your search by actively seeking out opportunities online. Generalized professional sites like LinkedIn can be highly beneficial because of their broad scope and name recognition across a variety of fields. **LinkedIn**

LinkedIn is the largest professional networking platform in the world, making it an invaluable tool for connecting with like-minded professionals, exploring potential board positions, and highlighting your personal expertise. As of 2023, the LinkedIn community includes thousands of universities, millions of companies, and nearly a billion users.

LINKEDIN USERS

OVER 930 MILLION INDIVIDUALS

61 MILLION COMPANIES

151,000 SCHOOLS

2.7 million organizations post on LinkedIn on a weekly basis.

Figure 7: LinkedIn connects individuals, companies, and schools via a centralized platform.

With LinkedIn's advanced search features, you can identify which organizations and professionals are already affiliated with advisory boards. Participating in industry-specific groups and discussions can also help you develop your network and potentially attract attention from board recruiters. If you notice that someone you know has already served on a board, you could reach out to ask for their input.

Personal Outreach and Building Relationships

Networking within your field or related domains can increase your chances of finding a position on an advisory board. When possible, attend industry conferences and sign up for events where you can interact with colleagues. If you're in a relatively remote or rural area, many events now offer a virtual option that still allows active discussion and engagement via video chat.

It's also a good idea to join trade associations or professional organizations in your discipline. For example, if you're an expert in digital currencies and assets, you might consider joining the Chamber of Digital Commerce or the Association for Digital Asset Markets. These groups work to influence their respective industries and promote collaboration among members.

Building relationships with other leaders in your field can help you access advisory board positions that aren't publicly advertised. Some openings may only be discussed through word of mouth in order to secure direct referrals. Meeting new people is also critical for expanding your online network. With more professional acquaintances and associates, there's a higher probability that someone will alert you to an opening or suggest your name to an organization.

Working on a Corporate Advisory Board

Just as universities have their own advisory boards, corporations and other for-profit companies utilize them as well. Although there are clear variations in the role and purpose of an advisory board in a business setting, the core mission is the same: helping an organization make informed choices.

Members of corporate boards use their expertise to ensure a business is making prudent decisions in the current market. The exact scope and purpose of a board may vary based on the organization's needs. A startup might need general guidance on how to create a sustainable business model, while a well-established brand may simply need advice about how to expand into a new field.

Imagine that a wireless internet and phone company is struggling with marketing. They might compile an advisory board of experts in marketing and technology to provide strategy recommendations. By drawing from a diverse pool of candidates, the company ensures it's covering as many angles and perspectives as possible, including those that might be missed by the current leadership.

A potential board candidate could be a market researcher who has experience working for a competitor in the past. That board member would have the required knowledge and expertise to advise on both marketing and the current market landscape for wireless services. They would also be able to leverage their existing contacts to understand more about customer preferences, trends, and how phone companies should position their products for the best possible outcome.

If the same company started experiencing issues with risk management, then they could pivot the scope of their advisory board to include specialists in that area. A risk management expert could assist the company with identifying potential risks and developing mitigating strategies. This might include analyzing market volatility, assessing supply chain disruptions, or advising about matters of regulatory compliance.

The board member's expert input would help the company proactively respond to risks and create contingency plans to ensure continuity of operations.

While some organizations choose to rotate board members according to their most pressing priorities, others establish more than one advisory board. The best setup depends on the size of your business, your ability to manage multiple boards, and whether your most significant concerns are functionally related. Including several types of experts together on the same board can help you keep a holistic picture of your company. At the same time, attempting to handle too many issues at once can result in a fractured, disjointed system.

Key Responsibilities

The exact responsibilities of advisory board members will be established by the overseeing organization. Some boards may have stricter rules about details like obligations, the frequency of meetings, and term lengths. Make sure you review all duties and negotiate as needed before accepting a position. Having to resign from the board early could reflect negatively on you while pursuing another role.

RESPONSIBILITIES OF CORPORATE BOARD MEMBERS

- Attend board meetings
- Advise company leaders about best practices
- Research emerging issues in the field
- Collaborate with other board members
- Support new initiatives and programs
- Set goals for the board
- Assess current company strategies

Figure 8: Corporate advisory board members handle a variety of administrative, technical, and strategic tasks.

In general, responsibilities typically include participating in meetings, analyzing the current state of your field, and offering guidance to company leadership. This may involve interfacing with other members of the organization or parts of your personal external network. You may even be asked to represent the company at official functions like industry conferences.

Meetings and Discussions

Advisory boards meet on a regular basis as determined by their governing policies. Some boards may only convene twice a year, while others may meet monthly. Although many companies have in-person meetings, holding them virtually makes recruitment easier since membership isn't constrained by geography.

In between sessions, members remain in communication to ensure they're informed about company activities and any potential issues that need to be discussed at the next meeting. For example, if you know the board intends to talk about new bills that have been proposed in the state legislature, you might look up the bills in question and any relevant precedents. Preparing extensively before meetings leaves more time for serious discussion instead of tabling issues to conduct more research later.

During the meeting itself, members can offer suggestions and feedback about topics on the agenda or ask clarifying questions from company representatives about current priorities. Members may also share updates about action items from the previous meeting, such as reaching out to an external connection or consulting with an employee.

After the meeting, advisory board members may spend some time debriefing amongst themselves or checking in with the company leadership. If advisors only come to a central location for occasional meetings, this time provides them with the chance to conduct one-on-one discussions in person.

Personal Networking

Even though advisory boards are group environments, most individual members spend a significant amount of time conducting personal networking and outreach. Networking allows board members to establish connections with other organizations on a personal level and as a representative of the company.

If you're new to an advisory board, networking may also involve internal introductions to company leaders and employees. Cultivating internal relationships will give you a stronger understanding of the company's goals, values, and needs. Learning more about the company makes it easier for you to tailor your recommendations and feedback.

Conducting Ongoing Research

Even if you're highly experienced in your field, a core responsibility of being a board member is to stay up to date on current events. This might involve reading industry publications, signing up for webinars, or evaluating formal reports about notable incidents. If you find something of interest, you can share the specifics with the board to engage in shared learning and promote open discussion.

You may even be asked to prepare responses on behalf of the company you represent. For example, regulatory authorities are often legally required to accept opinions and comments from the public while considering new rules. With few exceptions, federal agencies must allow 30 days for comments after publishing a proposed rule.

STAGES OF FEDERAL RULINGS

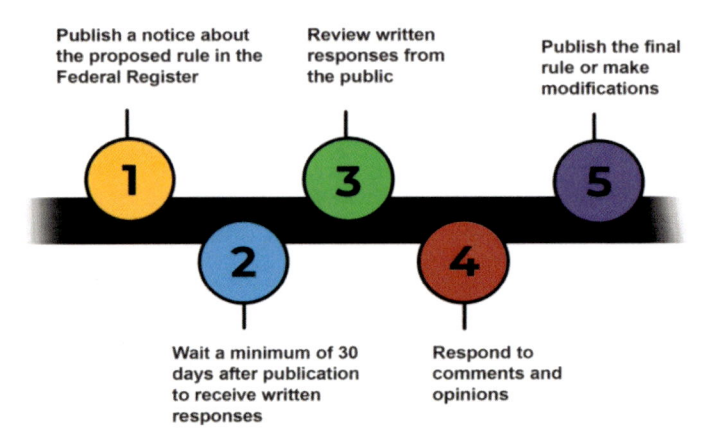

1. Publish a notice about the proposed rule in the Federal Register
2. Wait a minimum of 30 days after publication to receive written responses
3. Review written responses from the public
4. Respond to comments and opinions
5. Publish the final rule or make modifications

Figure 9: Proposed federal rulings must take into account comments and opinions from the public and industry.

Issuing a response from the board can influence future policy and affect whether regulators modify proposed rulings. If there's significant pushback from industry, labor, or the general public, federal agencies may even hold hearings to discuss the proposed legislation.

Looking Ahead

This chapter consisted of a deep dive into advisory boards and the professionals who join them. Along the way, you learned how to find open positions using platforms like LinkedIn and the best methods of determining whether an organization is reputable. We also explored what it's like to serve on a corporate advisory board as part of a for-profit entity.

The next chapter will discuss how to monitor emerging trends and apply lessons learned from throughout your industry. This will include several case studies from leading organizations like Adobe and

Amazon. Lastly, we will cover how to design program content and assist in curriculum design for ongoing education.

3

Leveraging Your Industry Experience and Insights

Working on an advisory board is a valuable opportunity to use your experience and expertise for the benefit of others. Whether you're volunteering at a university or receiving compensation on a corporate board, your insights can help shape the strategic direction of an entire organization. Serving on a board also gives you a unique vantage point that's likely to be different from your other roles.

Your experiences as a seasoned professional are particularly important when analyzing industry trends, current events, and the larger environment in which your organization operates. Since board members often come from different career paths, you might notice patterns forming or draw conclusions from data that others overlook.

However, not all trends are worth pursuing. It's important to distinguish between anomalies and long-term shifts that could have a lasting impact on your industry. Advisory board members can combine their individual knowledge to evaluate the staying power of emerging trends and decide whether there are any opportunities associated with recent changes to the market. Making this judgment call requires a deep understanding of your industry, the competitive landscape, and underlying social influences.

You should also keep an open mind about how technological advancements could alter your vision of the future. Many experts once doubted the long-term viability of online education, especially when online degrees were heavily stigmatized as less reputable than their in-person equivalents. Yet in the present, online instruction is widely recognized as a legitimate pathway to obtaining a degree or accessing continuing education. Experts who doubted remote learning didn't account for the expansion of technologies like video streaming, high-speed internet, and real-time captioning.

Understanding Obstacles and Risks in Context

In addition to identifying trends, board members must be attuned to how certain obstacles or risks affect specific groups. Location is a key consideration since challenges can specifically apply to different areas and have varying degrees of impact on affected organizations.

For example, a highly localized concern is unlikely to seriously disrupt operations for a major global corporation. Meanwhile, a global challenge that's represented in the majority of customer populations could be an existential threat. As an advisory board member, it's up to you to help organizations understand the broader implications of risk and suggest mitigating strategies.

Global Challenges

Challenges that occur on a global level don't always affect the entire world population. They may simply affect multiple regions or geographically dispersed areas at a significant rate that warrants consideration on an international scale. Global concerns might include widespread changes in behavior, disruption of traditional technologies, economic fluctuations, or armed conflicts.

The impact of a global risk or threat may be lessened if you're advising an organization with a strict local or national focus. At the same time, it might seem like a relatively insulated organization is unaffected when it's actually subject to subtle influences or chain reactions from events around the world.

A healthcare system in Kansas might not seem like it has much to do with natural disasters in Puerto Rico, but Hurricane Maria destroyed a factory in Puerto Rico in 2017 that supplied saline to many U.S. facilities. Because of the storm, there was a shortage of saline, which negatively impacted patient care all over the United States.

This example reinforces the importance of diversity and recruiting board members with unique backgrounds. While a healthcare system might not understand all the implications of a localized natural disaster, a business leader on their advisory board might have direct experience with continuity planning after emergencies. They could urge the healthcare system to check whether any essential supplies were sourced from that area, which would give them a vital head start in finding alternate suppliers before other facilities discovered the source of the shortage.

Regional Challenges

Regional risks or challenges affect more than one country in relatively close proximity to each other. This doesn't always follow traditional borders or continents. A regulation in the European Union could drastically alter member nations without impacting the continent of Europe as a whole. Similarly, slowing economic growth in one country could impact its neighbors due to cross-border commerce and employment.

Depending on how active your organization is in a given geographic area, a regional concern may not warrant any mitigating strategy other than monitoring the situation. However, it's always important to consider whether a regional issue is simply the first sign of a budding global trend.

National Challenges

Challenges at the national level can stem from economic policies, social influences, laws, and a host of other factors. For a global organization, tailoring operations to fit a single country can be expensive and difficult to implement. At the same time, many businesses are increasingly focused on personalization and catering to the needs of smaller demographic groups.

FACTORS IN ANALYZING NATIONAL CHALLENGES

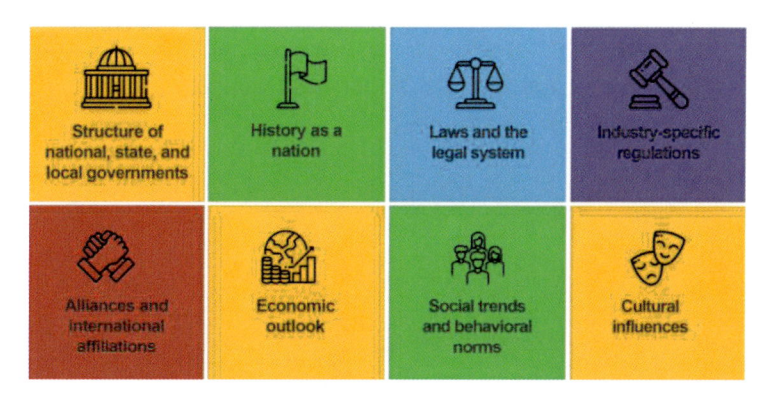

Structure of national, state, and local governments	History as a nation	Laws and the legal system	Industry-specific regulations
Alliances and international affiliations	Economic outlook	Social trends and behavioral norms	Cultural influences

Figure 10: National-level influences and regulations are highly complex and difficult to manage even for global entities.

As an advisor, you'll need to balance these competing priorities to determine what's feasible. While it might not be possible to offer country-specific products or services, you could recommend developing multiple options that would appeal to broader audiences than just American or Western consumers.

Local Challenges

Challenges that are more restricted in scale may include changing demographics, limitations in infrastructure, and availability of supply lines. Assessing the characteristics of local markets can guide your recommendations as you seek to identify new opportunities or promote your organization to local populations. Remember that even small communities can have an outsized impact on an industry or the demand for a given set of skills.

Palm Beach State College provides an intriguing example of how local areas can differ from the national norm. The school once offered degrees in sugar technology as part of the Sugar Technology Institute it launched in 2008. The program was developed in cooperation with U.S. Sugar, Florida Crystals, and the Sugar Cane Growers Cooperative of Florida due to the high prevalence of sugar-related industrial activity in the surrounding communities. Other partners included the Florida Office of the Governor and several nonprofits.

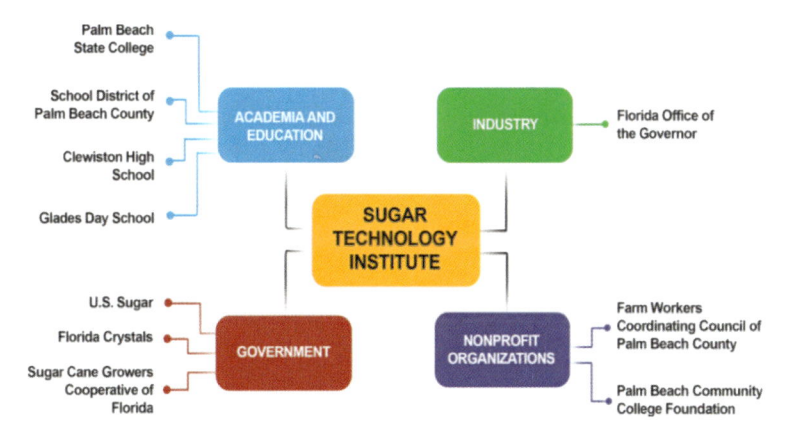

Figure 11: The Sugar Technology Institute is an example of an effective collaborative arrangement between organizations in different sectors.

The Sugar Technology Institute eventually evolved into the Industrial Skills Training Academy, a free three-year program sponsored by U.S. Sugar. The academy partners with leading companies such as Loctite and Mobil for specialized instruction. This reinforces how cooperative agreements between industry, nonprofit organizations, government, and academia can yield effective results for learners even in a highly localized context.

Case Studies and Lessons Learned

Many leaders abide by the common misconception that only learnings from within your own industry or sector are applicable to your organization. However, you don't need to work in the same functional area or have the same global reach to benefit from studying the underlying mechanisms of a case.

For example, the U.S. military has one of the most sophisticated instructional programs in the world. Even if you aren't part of a military entity, you can still learn from studying its structure, strategy, or mistakes.

Rather than concentrating on the type of organization, think about the type of problem and how those might present in your company or university.

When looking for commonalities or potential learnings from a case study, consider how your capabilities and business architecture overlaps with those of the subject in the study. If the company in the example is facing a problem related to strategy, you can assess the outcomes to see whether there are any useful recommendations to strengthen your organization's plan for the future.

Figure 12: Your organizational capabilities in a particular functional area won't always align with other companies' strengths and weaknesses. Consider the impact of these differences as you assess potential learnings from case studies.

Broadening your research can help you become a more informed advisor by sourcing information from a variety of industries. If each member of an advisory board finds different case studies, you're more likely to approach problems from multiple perspectives.

Amazon's Monitron System

Amazon is a large company with diversified interests, so internalmany of the problems it encounters can apply to multiple industries. Even if a proposed solution ends up being cost prohibitive for the organization you're advising, you can still derive value from studying how the world's biggest companies approach problem-solving.

Consider the following real-life situation. Prior to December 2020 when the Monitron system was announced, Amazon knew it needed to scale and optimize its maintenance. The retailer had hundreds of fulfillment centers to upgrade all over the world. As many as 80 engineers were involved in maintaining equipment at each location.

Amazon's leaders were struggling to find a way to cost-effectively improve equipment monitoring using techniques such as oil analysis and ultrasound. Technicians took manual readings in the field and analyzed the results themselves in order to determine the overall condition for a piece of equipment. This took far too much time.

Unsurprisingly, facilities would often experience unplanned stoppages when an issue occurred and a technician needed to determine the cause of the problem after the fact. Even relatively minor issues could have serious consequences for the schedule and order fulfillment. A single sorter going out of service for an hour could delay up to 10,000 orders.

Amazon first pursued the idea of implementing a predictive maintenance program to improve equipment reliability and optimize their maintenance plans. The company quickly discovered that those types of programs are extremely costly and require additional personnel to monitor the system and analyze the resulting data. The total expense was too high to justify the savings in time and efficiency.

After returning to the drawing board, Amazon decided to pursue an internal solution that could be operated by existing personnel. This led them to develop Monitron, a monitoring system that analyzes equipment for certain tell-tale signs of impending failure or malfunction. If vibration patterns or temperature indicate a piece of equipment isn't operating as intended, technicians can now proactively address the problem instead of responding after it breaks down.

Monitron incorporates machine learning to detect potential issues and predict the state of essential components like motors or bearings. It relies on a system of wireless sensors to capture data. These sensors can be easily installed by Amazon's existing technicians, which avoids the issue of needing to hire additional staff.

The company tested the system in Europe from August 2020 through May 2021. The Monitron pilot predicted that 68 pieces of equipment could fail within the 10-month period after analyzing 792 machines. The results were so promising that Amazon added the system to another 25 fulfillment centers before the end of 2021.

By upgrading their maintenance programs, Amazon was able to reduce unplanned equipment outages by 69 percent. The Monitron system receives updates from equipment every hour, which greatly shortens the amount of time to detect a potential failure. With manual techniques, it could take up to four weeks to realize there could be an imminent problem.

This case study showcases the importance of exploring unorthodox ideas and trying new methods instead of settling for a less-than-perfect solution. Amazon might have invested millions of dollars in Monitron technology to streamline operations, but you shouldn't get distracted by the cost. Instead, the key takeaway is that technological upgrades can increase efficiency, but you may need to test multiple solutions before finding the right one. This case study could lead your advisory board to think about creative applications of advanced technologies like machine learning even though there are obvious differences between Amazon and your organization.

Ryder's Customer Advisory Board Program

The transportation and supply chain management company Ryder maintains a Customer Advisory Board (CAB) to promote customer engagement. The company uses direct feedback to inform their strategy decisions. For example, insights from CAB research led to a marketing campaign that increased leads by 21 percent in a single month.

Furthermore, CAB helps drive innovation by aligning new products and services with customer needs. Ryder launched a vehicle-sharing network, developed a digital platform to enhance supply chain visibility, and extended service leases after reviewing data from CAB.

From a cultural standpoint, CAB encourages Ryder employees to keep the focus on the customer. This consistent push to leverage customer engagement has allowed Ryder's leadership to transform the company into a customer-centric organization. Ryder was even honored with a prestigious Loyalty360 award from The Association for Customer Loyalty because of its deep commitment to customers.

Ryder's success shows what your organization can accomplish with the support of advisory boards. Even a board with a narrow mandate has the potential to yield valuable insights that can change your goals and the trajectory of your overall strategy.

Adobe's Customer Advisory Board Program

The computer software company Adobe has a group of Customer Advisory Boards that includes hundreds of members all over the world. These individuals influence product strategy, analyze customer feedback, and provide their unique perspectives on market trends. Some CABs are centered around specific products, such as Adobe's Experience Cloud CAB, while others maintain a more holistic view of the organization.

In 2021, Adobe announced the creation of its first International Advisory Board. The group consisted of six founding members from distinct but accomplished backgrounds. To emphasize the crucial nature of having diverse perspectives, consider the differences between the career paths of these two members: Heizō Takenaka and Dr. Dieter Zetsche.

Dr. Heizō Takenaka is an economist and political figure who once served as the Japanese Minister of Economic and Fiscal Policy. He also teaches as a professor at Keio University in Tokyo. Meanwhile, Dr. Dieter Zetsche, established his career as a leader of automotive groups like Daimler AG. He was also the CEO and Head of Commercial Vehicles for Chrysler.

These two board members have drastically different histories, but Adobe chose them both to serve on the International Advisory Board. A group that's too homogenous may be limited in its insights or methodologies, so sourcing members from multiple industries is prudent to ensure you have a wealth of personal philosophies, experiences, and connections.

Curriculum Design and Program Content

Just like any other form of instruction, curriculum design plays a vital role in executive education by establishing a framework to organize course content. It ensures that key concepts are presented in a logical way and sets the overall learning objectives for the course. If a program isn't thoughtfully constructed, it could lead to poor performance and cause frustration among students.

As you consider various elements of the curriculum, bear in mind that there are many different philosophies that describe the process of learning. For example, David Kolb, an expert in education, developed his own model with four distinct stages: concrete experience, reflective observation, abstract conceptualization, and active experimentation.

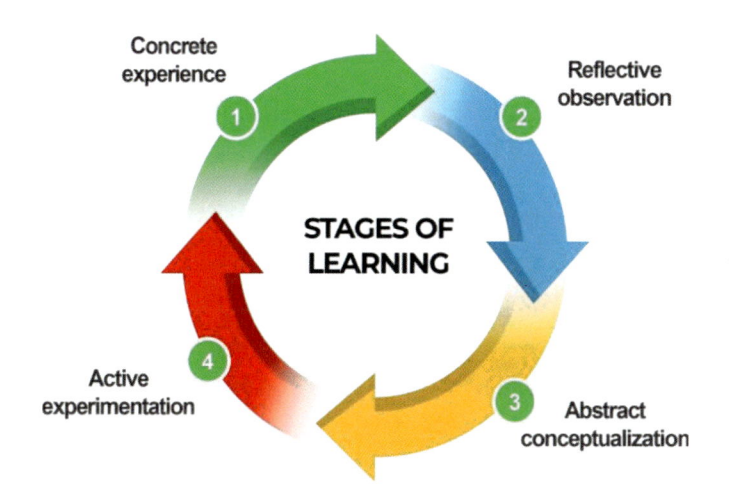

Figure 13: David Kolb's four-stage approach is one theory of learning among many.

In Kolb's model, students begin by relying on their emotions and feelings since they're unfamiliar with the situation and lack true understanding. From there, they progress into a watchful stage where they reflect on their observations. In the third stage, learners begin to apply theories and logical analysis to cultivate a deeper understanding of the topic. Lastly, they reach a period of active experimentation where they test different ideas and methods based on their personal knowledge.

It may be helpful to review these types of theories while compiling your thoughts about an executive education program at your institution. While it's challenging to address every potential style of learning, studying a broad range of methodologies will provide you with a strong foundation of knowledge for the future.

Curriculum Development and Program Design

Universities and academic institutions are likely to have their own approaches to curriculum and program design. If you're new to the advisory board, ask if there's an existing process or a preferred method to submit feedback about existing programs. Key considerations may include the following, among others:

- Target audience
- Style of learning (e.g., experiential)
- Number of courses
- Course offerings
- Program delivery (e.g., in person, online, or hybrid)
- Class and program size

Regardless of the exact structure, curriculum and program design follow the same general pattern of development. This process ensures that blocks of instruction are delivered in a methodical manner to satisfy all desired course outcomes.

Identifying Needs and Objectives

The first step is to identify students' needs and their reasons for seeking out instruction. For an executive education program, schools consider the skill sets required to effectively lead an organization. They may hold focus groups to test program elements or conduct surveys with executives to determine what executives hope to gain from educational experiences.

Effective programs will clearly articulate the learning objectives that align with the institution's values and students' needs. Like any other goal, these objectives should follow the SMART acronym and be specific, measurable, achievable, relevant, and time bound. Establishing desired outcomes in advance provides a roadmap for the design process and ensures that learners understand the core purpose of each course.

Establish Learning Parameters

In the next stage, you'll need to define the learning parameters for the program. This helps distinguish executive education courses from programs with different audiences, goals, or functions. After all, a mid-career executive who pursues continuing education has unique needs compared to a recent high school graduate studying business for the first time.

You must also take into account any limitations that impact the course. This might include time constraints, the availability of resources, class size, or the need for specific technologies. Balancing limitations against learning outcomes is crucial for creating a realistic, manageable curriculum.

Furthermore, the design plan should outline which instructional methods will be used to facilitate learning. This information not only makes it easier to develop courses, but it also allows students to anticipate whether they'll be successful with those forms of instruction. Someone who prefers simulations and experiential learning might avoid an executive education program that purely consists of lecture.

In general, it's best to have a blend of different instructional methods to enhance engagement and appeal to different preferences. This way, if someone dislikes group discussions, they might still enroll because the program description mentions guest speakers, individual research projects, and case studies.

You must also develop methods of evaluation to assess students' progress and quantify whether learning objectives are met. Options include traditional written tests, oral exams, individual or group projects, presentations, and practicums. Even in pass-fail or ungraded courses, periodic evaluations are important for learners to gauge their progress.

Incorporate Student Feedback

An effective executive education program will solicit feedback from students at the end of each course. Reviewing input from learners can help you see where improvements are needed, especially if there's a general consensus about which aspects of a course were lacking.

The Start-Stop-Continue technique is a popular method of gathering feedback in an open-ended way. Unlike numerical rating scales or multiple-choice questions, this process allows students to expand upon their thoughts with guided prompts. The Start-Stop-Continue technique uses unique framing to ask students what they liked, disliked, and would like to see in the future.

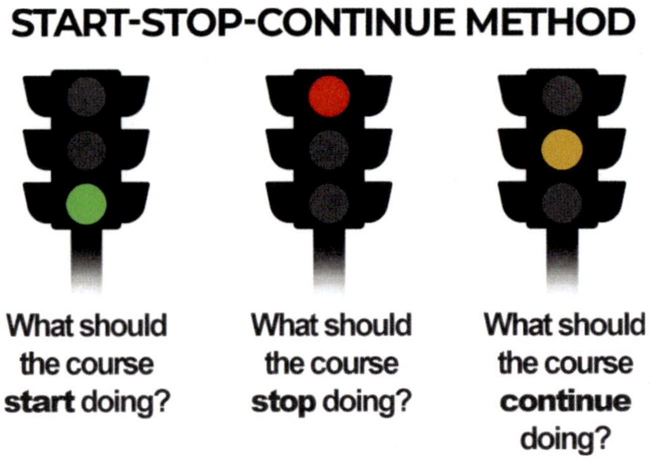

START-STOP-CONTINUE METHOD

| What should the course **start** doing? | What should the course **stop** doing? | What should the course **continue** doing? |

Figure 14: Open-ended questions like those used in the Start-Stop-Continue method encourage students to provide details and explain their thoughts about the program.

Course and program evaluations are distinct from instructor evaluations. Those may be conducted separately to assess the performance and behavior of a particular instructor. Regularly obtaining feedback from course participants can help curriculum designers and host institutions identify problems, improve content, and grow over time.

Industry Knowledge and Subject Matter Experts

Industry knowledge adds a real-world component to any curriculum, bridging the gap between theoretical concepts and practical applications. By integrating current industry trends and case studies, executive learners gain valuable insights that directly translate to their professional roles.

This approach fosters a deeper appreciation for executive decision-making and encourages students to evaluate case studies in the context of the real world. It means the difference between presenting students with a hypothetical situation on paper and showing them the actual ramifications of an executive's decision to reinforce course concepts.

Many executive education programs seek out subject matter experts (SMEs) who have specific skills or technical abilities that will benefit students. These individuals may act as guest speakers, mentors, or consultants to complement other forms of instruction. Their perspectives can add a fresh perspective to emerging trends and ensure that executive education courses remain relevant even in rapidly evolving industries.

Looking Ahead

Chapter Three expanded upon your existing knowledge of executive education programs and how they benefit modern leaders. Along the way, you learned about how to leverage your industry experience and assess local, national, regional, and global challenges in context.

In the next chapter, we'll delve into diversity, equity, and inclusion (DE&I). We'll discuss how to cultivate diverse applicant pools, remove barriers to access, and creative an inclusive culture. You'll also learn how some of the world's leading companies are currently handling DE&I initiatives.

4

Advocating for Diversity, Equity, and Inclusion

Diversity, equity, and inclusion are critical factors in driving organizational success both in business and in academia. DE&I is essential for achieving sustainable growth and ensuring executive education programs reflect the true nature of the real world. Your organization's commitment to DE&I should be apparent not only among instructors and advisors but also among the student body.

It all starts with recruitment. If candidates for your programs all have similar backgrounds and attributes, ask what steps the institution is taking to reach communities that have historically been excluded from higher execution. Cultivating a diverse applicant pool is more likely to yield varied perspectives in the classroom and ensure that executives from marginalized groups have equal access to the same educational opportunities.

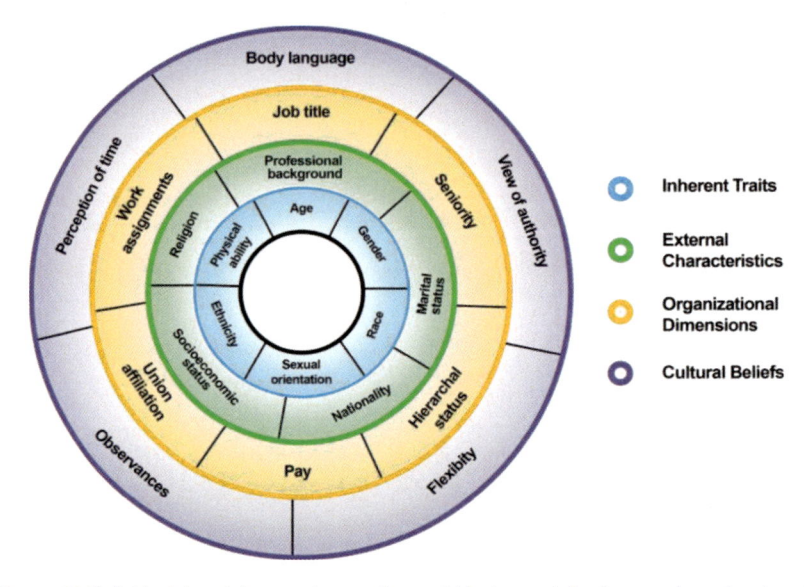

Figure 15: Individuals have inherent traits as well as variable characteristics that may change based on their circumstances or choices.

There are four overarching types of characteristics to consider while implementing DE&I initiatives: inherent traits, external characteristics, organizational dimensions, and cultural beliefs. Each category influences an individual's personality in different ways.

- Inherent traits are permanent facets of a person that they've had since birth.
- External characteristics are qualities that can change throughout someone's lifetime.
- Organizational dimensions include factors that distinguish people from one another in the context of a particular group.
- Cultural beliefs are defined by a person's worldview and community.

Creating a Legacy of Diversity, Equity, and Inclusion

In an inclusive learning environment, students are exposed to a multitude of perspectives that may challenge their current views about the world. Diversity of thought stimulates creative thinking and fosters a deeper understanding of complex global issues such as poverty and discrimination.

By championing DE&I within your program, you can develop executive leaders who are not only technically competent but also empathetic, emotionally intelligent, and culturally sensitive. These individuals will bring those traits back to their respective organizations, which contributes toward a more equitable future in business, nonprofit sectors, and government.

Furthermore, DE&I can have a positive impact on business performance. When executive teams embrace diversity, they better reflect the diversity of society, which makes the organization more sensitive to cultural nuances and the unique needs of different communities. A study conducted by the management consulting firm McKinsey & Company found that companies with greater executive diversity have a 25 percent higher likelihood of achieving revenue growth compared to their less diverse counterparts.

Diversity at the executive level also fosters a more welcoming workplace culture. When employees see that DE&I initiatives are more than just empty promises, they'll be more likely to become personally invested in promoting an inclusive environment. Employees who feel respected and valued on a deep level are more likely to be engaged, productive, and committed. In turn, this often leads to reduced attrition, higher employee satisfaction, and increased productivity.

In addition, an inclusive culture encourages employees to collaborate and use their creativity to tackle problems. When individuals recognize others will be receptive, there's a greater chance they'll feel comfortable sharing innovative ideas or making suggestions about a new approach.

Ongoing Support for Program Graduates

Even after students graduate from your executive education program, it's still imperative to offer support and DE&I resources. Alumni become informal ambassadors for your program, so they can benefit from ongoing communications about how to promote diversity and address systemic barriers within their respective industries. They may also have insights into how you can improve your application or selection process to make your program more accessible to marginalized communities.

Graduates from your program may even be interested in maintaining ongoing connections. For example, alumni could launch a mentorship program for executives from underrepresented backgrounds. Pairing up-and-coming leaders with mentors ensures they have access to external guidance beyond the traditional offerings of your program.

Another option to foster DE&I is to sponsor networking opportunities such as online alumni platforms or conferences. Networking enables leaders to expand their contacts, exchange ideas, and establish relationships with a broad range of peers. These types of interventions also give alumni the chance to participate in ongoing dialogues about diversity, equity, and inclusion with like-minded individuals.

Lastly, you can also establish student groups that uplift marginalized leaders or contribute to existing organizations with a focus on DE&I. For example, the Executive Leadership Council is a nonprofit that works to empower Black executives throughout their careers. If your program is brand new, extremely small, or otherwise unable to sponsor a variety of student groups, supporting entities like the Executive

Leadership Council through partnerships or donations is still a meaningful way to foster diversity at the executive level.

Inclusive Recruitment and Selection Practices

If you want to be committed to promoting inclusive recruitment and selection practices for executive education, then you need to believe that shifting your focus from simply reducing bias to actively promoting inclusivity is crucial in creating a learning environment that embraces diversity and empowers individuals from all backgrounds.

CREATING AN INCLUSIVE APPLICATION AND SELECTION PROCESS

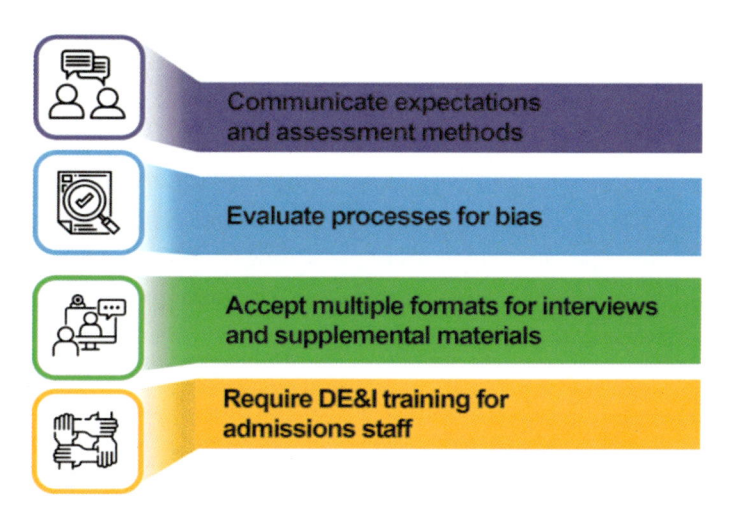

- Communicate expectations and assessment methods
- Evaluate processes for bias
- Accept multiple formats for interviews and supplemental materials
- Require DE&I training for admissions staff

Figure 16: Creating an inclusive application process requires a multi-pronged approach that addresses the potential for bias and improves accessibility.

By designing behavioral interventions, conducting background research, and incorporating current initiatives such as social norm messaging and intergroup contact, you can focus on cultivating an inclusive curriculum and programs that inspire and support leaders from diverse communities.

Establishing a Diverse Talent Pipeline

In order to create an executive education program that reflects DE&I principles, you first need to establish a recruitment pipeline to attract students. If your recruiting practices aren't accessible and inclusive, you won't have a diverse applicant pool to choose from.

If you don't see diversity reflected in your first round of candidates, it isn't a signal that executives from marginalized communities aren't interested in executive education. Instead, it should prompt you to consider your program elements, marketing, and communication. For example, if you hope to find more disabled executives who are interested in your university, using ableist language in advertising or failing to use accessibility features like alt text for photos will only inhibit your efforts.

Your organization needs to take deliberate steps to reach prospective candidates from underrepresented backgrounds by showing sensitivity and respect. This might include networking with minority-owned businesses about their needs or investing in scholarships for marginalized leaders.

Inclusive Selection and Admissions Processes

You should also examine whether your selection criteria are inclusive and equitable as you narrow your list of candidates. A diverse applicant pool doesn't automatically guarantee an inclusive or equitable process, especially if different teams are responsible for recruiting and making the final decisions about admissions.

Although strategies to mitigate bias and cultivate inclusivity should be tailored to your specific organization, there are several generalized best practices that can put your university on the right path. The following recommendations are far from a complete list of actions you can take to create a fairer environment for applicants. Identifying school-specific measures is up to you and your fellow leaders.

Communicate Expectations and Assessment Methods

Clearly state your organization's expectations for candidates and what constitutes a successful application. Not all applicants will necessarily have the same cultural understanding of professionalism or unspoken norms surrounding applications. For example, although it's now illegal to request a personal photograph on a candidate's resume, it used to be an established custom to require one in Germany.

If you address some of these concerns upfront, you can mitigate the chance that some candidates will misunderstand what they need to do to be successful. If you note that all applications will be viewed without names, locations, pictures, or other identifying information, then applicants will know there aren't hidden expectations surrounding their personal attributes.

Application instructions for your program should also delineate how candidates will be assessed and use specific qualifications. If one part of the application has particular weight, note that in a prominent place so that candidates understand the general scale. Use scores from standardized tests like the GRE with caution. Standardized tests are often biased against marginalized students.

Another key aspect of promoting inclusive recruitment and selection practices is how you construct evaluations and assessments. Traditional selection processes often rely on subjective judgments that can inadvertently perpetuate biases and limit opportunities for underrepresented individuals. Objective evaluation criteria and rubrics make the process more transparent and promote the use of data-driven selection.

This enables candidates to showcase their skills on equal footing without worrying about subjective judgments like what counts as a professional appearance. For example, in 2010, a company called Catastrophe Management Solutions rescinded a job offer because the applicant—a Black woman named Chastity Jones who was qualified for the position in every way—refused to cut off her locs when asked. The company stated they felt her locs could "get messy."

Even though the Equal Employment Opportunity Commission lost a lawsuit on her behalf and later lost an appeal, the question of whether an admissions practice is inclusive of diverse cultures and communities is entirely separate from the law. In this case, Jones was targeted by an unfair idea of professionalism that limited opportunities for Black women with natural hair. The CROWN Act ("Creating a Respectful and Open World for Natural Hair") would later pass in numerous states, prohibiting employers from race-based discrimination against natural hairstyles such as locs or braids.

Evaluate Processes for Bias

An effective DE&I evaluation will also encompass your public-facing materials and communications. This includes your website, advertising, and any platforms students may need to navigate as they apply to your executive education program. Examine phrasing, images, and other elements to ensure all materials are free of bias.

If your application instructions are full of gendered language and the images on your website only show men, then you're sending the message that women aren't the intended audience for your program. It perpetuates the stereotype of men in leadership positions and dissuades women from applying, regardless of whether that was your intention.

Accept Multiple Formats for Interviews and Supplemental Materials

Some application processes involve interviews or submitting supplemental materials such as a portfolio or personal statements. When possible, provide multiple options to satisfy these requirements and allow candidates to select which ones are most conducive to their individual needs.

Stating that your organization is flexible about the format of application materials demonstrates that you're open to accommodations and making adjustments. This bolsters DE&I efforts by making it easier for many types of people to send in applications. Someone who works in remote areas with unpredictable infrastructure might struggle to coordinate a live video interview. Meanwhile, a blind candidate may prefer to record verbal statements instead of written ones.

It's also beneficial to designate points of contact for applicants who need additional assistance or clarification. This could be as simple as listing the contact information for the admissions office or a student advocate. Remember to include multiple methods of contact. Email may be more accessible for some applicants than calling an office during limited business hours in a specific time zone.

Require DE&I Training for Admissions Personnel

Before any employees, instructors, or advisory board members interact with the selection process, they should undergo DE&I training to ensure they're aware of best practices and common barriers that marginalized learners may face. Not only does this increase awareness of DE&I topics, but it also encourages staff to engage in continuous learning about diversity.

Diversity Among Instructors and Staff

Although many of the aforementioned recommendations are intended to address the admissions process for students, it's also important to consider diversity among instructors and staff. When marginalized students see themselves represented among the instructor population, it reinforces your organization's commitment to cultivating diversity at all levels.

Unfortunately, statistics from higher education still show room for significant improvement in academia. According to a 2020 study by the National Center for Education Statistics, white men and white women made up 51 percent and 28 percent, respectively. Black men and Black women, by comparison, only made up 2 percent each.

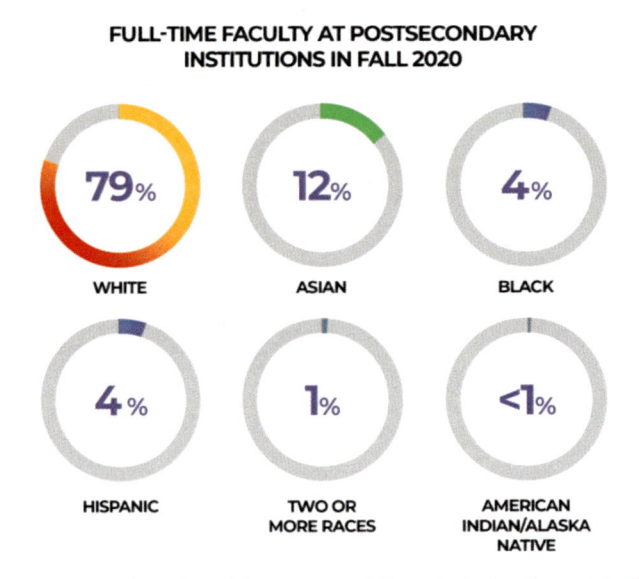

FULL-TIME FACULTY AT POSTSECONDARY INSTITUTIONS IN FALL 2020

79% WHITE	12% ASIAN	4% BLACK
4% HISPANIC	1% TWO OR MORE RACES	<1% AMERICAN INDIAN/ALASKA NATIVE

Figure 17: Gender and racial diversity among full-time faculty is still severely lacking.

These findings demonstrate why it's essential to consider intersectionality in hiring. Two people who share a single demographic group can still have vastly different lived experiences. For example, a Black man and a white man will have unique perspectives and face different systemic barriers even though both are men.

Therefore, individuals who are involved in hiring for executive education programs must consider intersectional diversity in context. This requires decision-makers to acknowledge the multifaceted nature of diversity and how specific marginalizations affect candidates who apply for instructor roles.

Conducting Research and Updating Perspectives

As your program continues, course content and instructional methods should be periodically reviewed to verify they're up to date. Current events, recent research findings, or new methodologies will undoubtedly appear over time. These changes will also have an impact on how your organization supports DE&I.

For example, you might have a strong understanding of bias in recruiting from leading an initiative at one of your companies before joining a university advisory board. But if the university is contemplating whether to use artificial intelligence to screen applications, you might not have relevant experience if those types of AI tools weren't in widespread use the last time you spearheaded a major initiative.

Periodically conducting a thorough review of how your personal experiences relate to present-day issues allows you to identify gaps in your knowledge as early as possible. If you encounter a subject you don't fully understand, you can take steps to learn more and stay informed about emerging issues that may hinder equal access to executive education. This makes you a better advisor and contributes to an organizational culture of self-accountability and personal growth.

Ensuring an Inclusive and Equitable Learning Environment

After addressing potential barriers and sources of bias in recruiting and selection, the next step is to evaluate the learning environment itself. In order to create an inclusive and equitable learning environment, it's vital to integrate DE&I principles into your instructional design process from start to finish. This involves carefully considering the content, resources, and activities in each course.

Incorporating a range of perspectives, examples, and public figures into your coursework encourages students to think broadly as they approach key concepts. For example, instead of only including case studies about American companies, analyze how different cultures and countries approach leadership. Not only does this acknowledge the diversity in the world, but it also teaches cultural sensitivity in a time of increasing globalization.

Different Teaching Styles

An effective instructor understands how to create an inclusive classroom atmosphere where every person feels respected and heard. Student-centered approaches support DE&I initiatives by fostering active participation and open dialogue within the classroom. This style of instruction encourages students to express their distinct opinions and share their perspectives in a space that celebrates diversity of thought.

However, it's important to use a range of different instructional techniques to properly communicate course concepts. For example, the Socratic style relies heavily on discussion and free exploration with the instructor serving as a facilitator. But not all lessons lend themselves well to a Socratic, dialogue-based model, especially when learners are interacting with a topic for the first time.

TEACHING STRATEGIES

FACILITATOR	AUTHORITATIVE	DELEGATING
O Emphasizes discussion	O Focuses on the instructor	O Centers students
O Allows students to explore	O Provides information in a direct way	O Promotes independent discovery
O Guided by instructor	O Minimizes student participation	O Applies to individual and group tasks
O Encourages student participation		

Figure 18: Various teaching strategies have different focus areas and levels of student participation.

Therefore, it may be necessary to use a more direct and authoritative mode in some cases. An authoritative style is highly traditional. It involves an instructor providing information to students through lecture or readings. Students only participate in the process by absorbing the information and taking notes.

Instructors may also delegate learning, which blurs the lines between Socratic discussions and direct lecture. With this style of learning, instructors introduce assignments and allow students to work independently on either individual or group tasks. They're available as a resource if anyone needs help or clarification about the work, but they take a less active role in the learning process.

Removing Barriers to Accessibility

Ensuring accessibility is an essential aspect of creating an inclusive and equitable learning environment. Instructional designers must be proactive by identifying and eliminating barriers in the planning stages. This process may involve evaluating course materials, consulting with accessibility experts, and implementing new technologies to support disabled executives in your program.

Accessibility can apply to the learning environment in more than one way. Accessibility considerations should include the following:

- Physical spaces that easily accommodate mobility aids
- Descriptive alt text to explain what's taking place in online photographs, images, or graphics
- Websites that are free of flashing lights and automation
- Warnings on potentially triggering content
- Captioning or sign language interpretation for live lectures
- Transcripts for recorded notes
- Accommodations requested by individual students or instructors

This is far from a complete list of accessibility considerations you should have for your executive education program. If you aren't sure how to improve accessibility, there are many resources and guides available through programs like Harvard University's Digital Accessibility Services portal.

Figure 19: Alt text should be descriptive enough to fully explain the purpose and content of an image.

Accessibility must be an ongoing endeavor that encompasses both physical and online learning environments. An effective DE&I

program should also have mechanisms in place to address complaints and accessibility-related requests in a timely manner with minimal disruption to the student.

Creating an Inclusive Culture

The classroom environment is more than just a physical or virtual space. It's also influenced by behaviors and social norms from the overall group. An inclusive culture is built on respectful dialogue, active listening, and empathy between participants. This allows students to openly engage and share their thoughts without fear of retaliation, ridicule, or discrimination.

Since executive education programs are aimed toward individuals with established careers, they blur the lines between traditional academic settings and the workplace. Therefore, many of your interventions to address cultural habits may need to be tailored to reflect this hybrid state. Many students will be accustomed to corporate environments, so they may be less familiar with how to use purely academic resources like student advising.

The culture of your program extends beyond the time spent in the classroom. Students may communicate on their own through platforms like LinkedIn, especially if group projects are part of your curriculum. If students encounter microaggressions or bias during informal conversations, they may not feel safe continuing the program. While you can't always control how people will behave when instructors aren't watching, you can establish strong social expectations and reporting mechanisms to address behaviors that conflict with a healthy culture.

Remember that the longevity of your organization's program depends on its ability to effectively implement DE&I initiatives and react quickly to any negative trends identified in periodic evaluations of DE&I performance. In a 2022 study by Staffing Industry Analysts, 75 percent of Gen Z respondents noted they would reconsider applying to a position if they weren't satisfied with the company's DE&I activities. This confirms that employees and leaders from Gen Z are increasingly aware of whether organizations are fostering a culture of diversity and acceptance.

Looking Ahead

This chapter was devoted to the concepts of diversity, equity, and inclusion. We explored various strategies to implement DE&I initiatives and identify the needs of underrepresented groups. This included a discussion on how to build diverse applicant pools and ensure selection processes are fair, equitable, and objective.

In the following chapter, we'll dive deeper into the relationships between academia and industry. You'll learn more about the elements of an effective partnership and how to manage cross-disciplinary teams in a variety of settings. We'll also review case studies of how other organizations balance business needs and executive education.

5

Collaborations Between Academia and Industry

Executive education is an intriguing subset of academia since it caters to adult learners with years of experience in their disciplines. Many students will be deeply connected to industry, and their last experiences with academia may have been decades in the past while pursuing undergraduate or graduate degrees. Because of this dual nature, executive education provides a unique opportunity for academic and industry to come together in support of shared goals.

Industry case studies, applied research, and academic theory serve as pillars of executive education programs. The various groups in collaborative agreements each have their own stakeholders and interests to protect. They also contribute different elements to the whole and dovetail in distinct ways with other participating organizations.

In collaborations between academia and industry, universities offer their research capabilities, educational resources, funding, and reputation. In return, they remain relevant within industry and secure connections that allow them to assess the needs of prospective students. These partnerships serve as an avenue for academic institutions to strengthen their curriculum and gain access to real-world insights beyond what you and your peers can provide as a small cohort of advisors.

Meanwhile, businesses benefit from the relationship by accessing cutting-edge research, developing a network of academic contacts, and improving their reputation by allying with prestigious schools. Not only can businesses gain additional knowledge by partnering with academic teams, but they can also make key discoveries by pooling financial resources. This is particularly valuable if an academic institution has funding available through grants or other means beyond corporate contributions from the company.

Your role as an advisor is to help design and deliver educational experiences that reflect academic concepts and industry trends. Advisory boards act as a bridge between the university and partnering entities. You may be asked to liaison between organizations, guide your institution's programs, or share your expertise about forming joint ventures.

Figure 20: Each entity in a collaboration contributes different elements to the whole.

Lastly, there are third-party entities that intersect with each of these groups since their products are related to the delivery or design of education. For example, Blackboard Learn is an online application that allows businesses, universities, and other organizations to develop their own learning environments.

Companies that specialize in educational technology services provide the applications and platforms for many executive education programs. Just a few of Blackboard Learn's partners include Rutgers University, Ohio University, and George Brown College. Their role in education is often overlooked, but they provide a critical network of services for distance and computer-based education.

Customized Educational Solutions

Although many collaborations between academia and industry result in generalized programs, there are also partnerships that focus on developing educational programs for specific organizations or industries. Individual companies may pursue standing relationships with academic institutions to establish a talent pipeline, encourage networking, or develop instructional content for internal use. Meanwhile, businesses in the same industry may band together to teach niche skills or encourage more young people to enter a field with declining workforce participation.

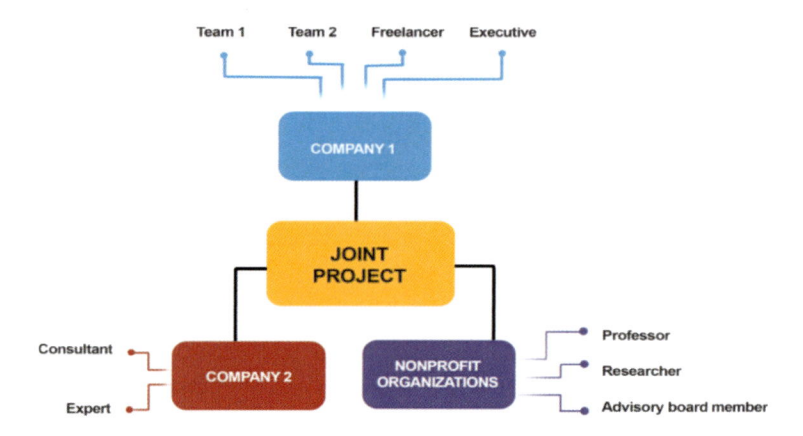

Figure 21: Multiple companies and nonprofit organizations may periodically collaborate on joint initiatives.

In 2022, Google announced a joint initiative with the University of Michigan to create a new industry specialization built on the Coursera platform. The program was designed to help graduates of the Google Career Certificate expand upon their existing skills by completing the Data Analytics in the Public Sector with R Specialization from the University of Michigan. Alumni of the program also gain access to Google's consortium of over 150 organizations to seek out employment opportunities, including ones outside of Google.

Applied Research and Models of Innovation

Applied research bridges the gap between theoretical concepts and actual practice in the real world. Findings provide evidence-based insights that students can apply in their studies or their respective organizations. Ideally, the use of the most recent research ensures that executive education programs remain current while simultaneously introducing even seasoned executives to theoretical approaches they may not have encountered in the past.

However, creating true partnerships between academia and industry remains a challenge because of fundamental disconnects in how these two distinct spheres overlap. As an advisory board member, it's partially your responsibility to facilitate joint interactions and identify common ground where needed.

COMMON SOURCES OF FRICTION BETWEEN ACADEMIA AND INDUSTRY

Differing techniques or philosophical approaches	Relevance and practicality of ideas to real-world situations	Target audiences of research (i.e., academic vs. industrial research)
Social norms and behaviors among each group	Availability of resources and funding opportunities	Varying levels of openness to change
	Ability to tolerate risk	

Figure 22: Academia and industry have fundamentally different purposes that can cause friction during collaborative projects.

In 2022, a team of researchers from Sir Syed University of Engineering and Technology and Bahria University in Karachi, Pakistan, proposed a new model: the Academia-Industry Collaboration Plan (AICP). The AICP acknowledges that partnerships between academia and industry are limited by the former's desire to discover new theoretical approaches and the latter's preoccupation with profitability. However, the authors of the AICP also noted that collaboration is on the rise, especially in high-risk fields such as the pharmaceutical industry and information technology.

The research from these two universities proposes that the AICP can complement the triple helix model of innovation. This model combines industry, the government, and universities to drive innovative thinking. The three components contribute unique elements to the partnership that mitigate some of the drawbacks of each individual group in isolation.

Smoothing the differences between academia and industry requires more collaboration than a single joint venture between one or two organizations can accomplish, but even smaller achievements shift each category closer in the right direction. With this in mind, advisors and other intermediaries who facilitate partnerships between academia and industry must have a strong understanding of these stumbling blocks in order to suggest viable solutions. Many of these issues are systemic and unlikely to change without an external challenge.

For example, a professor and researcher who has built their career on theoretical methods isn't likely to be receptive to the idea that their work lacks practicality. Industry leaders, on the other hand, may be hesitant to let go of tried-and-true techniques that have already proven to be effective in the business world. Yet when these collaborative projects are successful, combating the long-held viewpoints of each group can result in innovative strategies and breakthroughs that wouldn't have otherwise been possible.

Establishing Roles and Responsibilities in Joint Ventures

Establishing the roles and responsibilities of each partner in a joint project reduces confusion and improves accountability for tracking major milestones. Each entity can further distribute its overall responsibilities by delegating tasks among its internal teams. Maintaining role clarity at all levels streamlines the flow of work and avoids the accidental duplication of efforts, but achieving true role clarity remains a challenge for a surprising percentage of organizations.

According to a 2019 report by the HR consulting firm Effectory, only 53 percent of employees feel they have enough role clarity in their current positions. This is a notable trend since the individuals who do have sufficient role clarity are 27 percent more effective. There's a significant drop in both efficiency and productivity when employees are unsure about their exact obligations.

Increasing the size of the joint initiative and including multiple larger organizations under the umbrella of a single project only further complicates matters. Task management software such as Asana or Airtable can assist with tracking and monitoring. Designated personnel from each organization can update these systems as needed to better facilitate cross-disciplinary cooperation.

Investing time and effort into improving role clarity greatly benefits overall project outcomes. Effectory's study reports that 75 percent of employees with clear roles are more passionate about their jobs compared to employees whose positions need more definition. This suggests that better role clarity increases buy-in and personal investment at significant rates.

Promoting an Inclusive Culture

An inclusive culture is an essential element of any successful team, but it's particularly important when multiple organizations are working together on shared initiatives. In these types of situations, each contributing group will have its own distinct internal culture. Over time, a secondary culture will develop among participants in the joint venture that's separate from the parent entities.

This is similar to how governments cooperate in shared organizations. From the World Health Organization to the International Space Station, participating nations must put aside some of their own behaviors and norms to support a mutual interest. A healthy working environment shows respect for different perspectives while reinforcing the culture of the joint initiative over those of individual contributing organizations.

The multinational law firm Pinsent Masons recommends using policies to drive alignment and a common purpose when integrating multiple organizations into a single team. This includes examining discrepancies in corporate culture and informal attitudes toward considerations like time. Anticipating these potential clashes makes it easier to standardize with formal procedures or provide training to emphasize expectations.

Finally, celebrating achievements can serve the dual purpose of recognizing the contributions of team members and reinforcing which behaviors are viewed as desirable by the joint venture. Showing appreciation also fosters a positive working environment and boosts morale about what a cross-functional team can accomplish.

Cross-Disciplinary Initiatives

Collaborating with external organizations strengthens your executive education programs and increases your ability to network broadly on behalf of your university. Practical insights from industry can ground theoretical principles from academia, ensuring that the most recent findings are practical and realistic. Meanwhile, academia provides a solid theoretical basis for industry leaders to innovate and test new practices in the real world.

While it may seem like university programs and businesses in the same general field will have a better understanding of each other's work, it can actually limit open exploration and stifle creative thought. Partnerships that involve cross-disciplinary cooperation across multiple disciplines ensure that students, advisors, and other stakeholders are continuously challenged by outside perspectives from different fields. Students in executive education programs that only maintain a narrow focus won't have the benefit of considering how other industries operate.

Cross-disciplinary cooperation also establishes a pathway for cutting-edge academic research to affect practices in a wide variety of industries. As more and more businesses learn about new techniques and research findings, they're more likely to test those approaches and modify their behaviors if they see a competitive advantage from updating their current methods. Not only does this ensure businesses are up to date on the latest techniques, but it also shortens the gap between theory and practice.

Building cross-disciplinary relationships with other organizations isn't restricted to major corporations. Small businesses and startups can use partnerships to enhance a limited workforce, gain a better understanding of related disciplines, or amplify specific capabilities. Collaborative agreements between entities of vastly different sizes is especially common in scientific fields where a startup or small business may have a highly technical specialty that's rare to find elsewhere.

For instance, in 2018, the pharmaceutical company Pfizer established an ongoing partnership with a German startup called BioNTech to develop a new type of flu vaccine. Despite its much smaller size, BioNTech was crucial to the endeavor because it had specialized knowledge about mRNA molecules. Coupled with Pfizer's experience with vaccine development and regulations, it made for a successful relationship.

This collaborative effort would eventually lead these two organizations to develop the mRNA-based COVID vaccine after the outbreak of the pandemic in 2020. Pfizer also sought out additional partners to expand its team, eventually including government agencies, the Rega Institute for Medical Research, and individual experts from universities all over the world. It even established ties with UPS to facilitate cold storage during transportation and Zipline to deliver vaccines to remote areas using drone technology.

While a global health emergency is an extreme situation, this example highlights what's possible when cross-disciplinary teams work together in pursuit of shared goals. Without the input of all these entities, Pfizer would have experienced drastically reduced capabilities in design, logistics, and regulatory compliance. By pooling knowledge and resources, this collaboration resulted in the rapid development of a complex medical intervention that would have taken much longer for Pfizer to create on its own.

Creating Effective Teams

A cross-functional team brings together a collection of individuals who have unique skill sets from different areas of business or different industries. Participants may also be from various levels within their respective organizational structures. A senior finance executive could end up working closely with an intern from a nonprofit.

Because of these differences, there are some best practices for you to consider as you compile teams or join one as a member. The key is to identify common ground wherever possible by establishing shared priorities, analyzing internal processes, and communicating openly about priorities like budgeting. Behnam Tabrizi, a Stanford University professor and an expert in executive education, discovered that nearly 75 percent of all cross-functional teams have dysfunctional workflows due to lack of standardization.

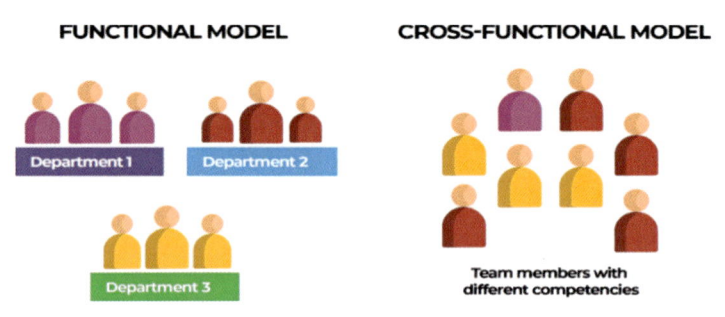

Figure 23: In a cross-functional model, team members often have different approaches, methods, and viewpoints.

Therefore, it's prudent to analyze policies in advance to anticipate clashes instead of reacting after an issue has been identified. For example, if your university uses an internal software to complete tasks, make sure the resulting materials can be converted for general use if they need to be shared outside your organization. If a company in a technical industry is accustomed to 24-hour time and the metric system, it could cause confusion to others who aren't familiar with those formats. Even these relatively minor disruptions can cause frustration and erode the cooperative spirit of the group.

BEST PRACTICES FOR BUILDING CROSS-FUNCTIONAL TEAMS

- Establish shared goals and priorities
- Choose employees who are flexible and open to change
- Use standardized tools and technology
- Replace team members who fail to collaborate
- Formalize policies as needed to address cultural differences
- Identify a method to track and monitor tasks
- Maintain a centralized budget to promote transparency

Figure 24: When building cross-functional teams, it's prudent to establish common methods and standardized processes as early as possible.

You may also need to create shared digital spaces to collaborate if members of the team aren't able to meet in person. Digital platforms like Zoom make it easy to hold meetings and discuss issues, but they aren't effective for tracking the completion of tasks or exchanging data. More than likely, you'll need multiple applications to be successful, and some trial and error may be required to find the best system for all.

Looking Ahead

In Chapter Five, we discussed the role of collaborative agreements and how they drive innovation. We reviewed how partnerships between academia and industry have formed throughout history and analyzed common sources of friction between these two distinct groups. We rounded out the chapter by examining cross-functional teams and how to effectively manage them.

Chapter Six will consider various strategies to sustain executive education programs and ensure that they remain relevant over time. This section of the book will also delve into administrative matters such as finance, marketing, and the responsible use of personal data.

6

Program Growth and Sustainability

Like any other university program, there are administrative considerations associated with executive education courses beyond the design and delivery of the content itself. Academic institutions must also market the program, retain faculty, and attract new students for each evolution. Together, these elements ensure that the program is sustainable, profitable, and able to evolve as needed over time.

Faculty members may find opportunities with your program through traditional means such as job boards, or they may hear about openings through word of mouth within their social circles. When advertising faculty positions or pursuing a particular instructor, it's essential to highlight any unique aspects of your courses that may help your school stand out from others.

For example, The University of Chicago Booth School of Business offers an executive education program with a specialization in finance. This short-term program is held over the course of several days on location in Chicago. An instructor or guest speaker who has limited time and already resides in the area may be more likely to accept this role over a competing offer to teach a multi-week program in another city.

EFFECTIVE MESSAGING AND ADVERTISING

- Focus on the program's unique offerings and how it provides value
- Emphasize the practical applications and tangible outcomes of enrolling
- Identify your target audiences
- Highlight faculty members and advisors who add credibility and prestige to your program
- Tailor your marketing materials to match the platform (e.g., Instagram vs. a school website).
- Use statistics and concrete details
- Showcase recent alumni and how the program enhanced their careers

Figure 25: *Marketing materials should showcase the major strengths of your program and appeal specifically to your target audience.*

In terms of attracting prospective students, messaging should focus on the program's unique offerings and how it addresses specific professional needs. Emphasize the practical relevance, real-world applications, and tangible outcomes of the program. Appealing to a particular audience can also make your marketing more compelling by highlighting how your program will benefit certain audiences. For instance, your courses may be tailored toward new executives with under five years of experience in their current roles.

Alumni achievements and faculty accomplishments can also serve as powerful testimonials to the strength of your program. Executives who see how others have benefited from your executive education are more likely to imagine how they might benefit as well. Highlighting faculty experiences also proves that you have access to a network of experts and prominent figures in the field.

Collectively, these measures can convince prospective applicants to reach out for additional information. These individuals may not be sure about pursuing continuing education, but this interaction still provides an additional touchpoint for you to establish a relationship with them. Even if they don't decide to enroll for the upcoming session, they're more likely to remember your program in the future when they do decide to take that next step.

Maximizing Your Personal Branding

Even though your main objective as an advisor is to enrich the program and assist the university, serving in an advisory role also allows you to build upon your personal brand. Being affiliated with a university increases your credibility and reputation as a recognized expert in your field. This may lead to future opportunities such as speaking engagements or promotions.

One of the most effective ways to build your brand and increase the visibility of the program is to leverage the power of social media. Sharing relevant updates, articles, and personal insights about various courses allows you to engage with the public and cultivate online relationships with your followers. Since most conversations on social media are publicly accessible, industry professionals or colleagues may notice that you're emerging as a leading voice in your field.

Figure 26: The value of social media lies in how much it compounds your reach and allows you to access not only your own network but also those of your contacts.

Brunswick Group, a strategic advisory firm, issues a Connected Leadership report to show how executives are using social media and characterize the public's response. In 2022, the firm surveyed 2,800 people who read financial publications and 3,600 employees from mid-sized and large companies. Brunswick Group also interviewed 16 leaders and their teams in detail to derive insights about digital connection.

The results are unsurprising in a world that increasingly relies upon digital communications and online spaces. Employees are four times more likely to support a CEO who uses social media and digital platforms. Among people who read financial publications, 86 percent of respondents believe it's important for leaders to communicate via online platforms.

These findings underscore the value of maintaining an online platform to network, communicate, and offer a genuine glimpse into your current role. A personal brand is just that—personal. If you fail to show your thoughts and feelings as an individual, you may seem unapproachable, untrustworthy, or inauthentic.

Building Interest Among Prospective Students

The effectiveness of any outreach program centers on its ability to reach and engage with a target audience in pursuit of a particular objective. For executive education programs, this goes far beyond superficial advertising or a simple call to action. Even short programs or distance education require time, money, and effort from executives who already have so many demands on their personal bandwidth.

Cultivating interest in your program requires a distinct selling point and value proposition that executives won't be able to match through other means. Whether it's advancing to a higher position or increasing their name recognition within the industry, your outreach efforts need to lay out the exact pathway executives can follow to achieve their career goals.

Internal Promotion

If you're serving as an advisor while also working for another organization, you can engage in internal promotion to advertise your university's executive education courses. Peers and colleagues are more likely to be interested since you have a personal stake in the program. If they have any questions, you're an easy point of contact to consult with.

Internal channels of communication can be an effective method of disseminating information throughout your company. Internal message boards, chat groups, and newsletters are all potential avenues to communicate with your fellow executives and company leaders. Posting information about the university will increase awareness about the program itself while simultaneously reinforcing the value of executive education as a whole.

If your company has a training department, you may be able to integrate information about the program into existing messaging about continuing education resources. The same applies to human resources, especially if your business offers tuition assistance for professional development. This approach ensures that employees in those departments have the details on hand if an executive or leader gets in touch to inquire about educational opportunities.

Advisors can also host informational sessions or short seminars to answer questions and generate excitement about the program. This works better if you belong to a large organization with many people who might be interested in executive education. Scheduling these events within the normal work day increases the likelihood that executives will be available to attend.

Making Enrollment Easy and Convenient

Another way to build interest in your executive education programs is by making the initial enrollment process as convenient as possible. If prospective students see that the application process is long or complicated, it could deter them from investigating further. Once you make a negative first impression, it'll be even more challenging to bring those individuals back to the table for additional discussions in the future.

Embracing online enrollment can streamline the process of applying and eliminate the need for physical paperwork. Your university probably has a centralized enrollment system already in place, but it's important to verify that specialized programs like executive education are also handled on the same platform. Evaluate the system to see if it's intuitive and easy to use. If you notice any opportunities to improve, include that in a list of recommendations from the advisory board.

Furthermore, the institution's website should provide clear and concise information about the program. This should include detailed descriptions of coursework, scheduling options, and whether any prerequisites are needed. If your university's executive education programs have already been operating for some time, analyze common questions and concerns to develop a section for frequently asked questions. An FAQ section allows prospective applicants to quickly find answers on their own without having to contact the university.

If your program has fixed deadlines for applications and enrollment, ensure the website clearly states when application materials are due. If you're personally assisting someone, send them reminders if you think they may forget about important dates. The school itself should also send out a reminder in advance of major deadlines to keep candidates informed.

Creating an Efficient Payment Process

The cost of an executive education program varies widely, so the exact expenses associated with enrollment should be listed somewhere on the program page. This helps avoid any surprises or accusations that the university is charging hidden fees. Making a sample budget or a list of costs removes any ambiguity from the situation.

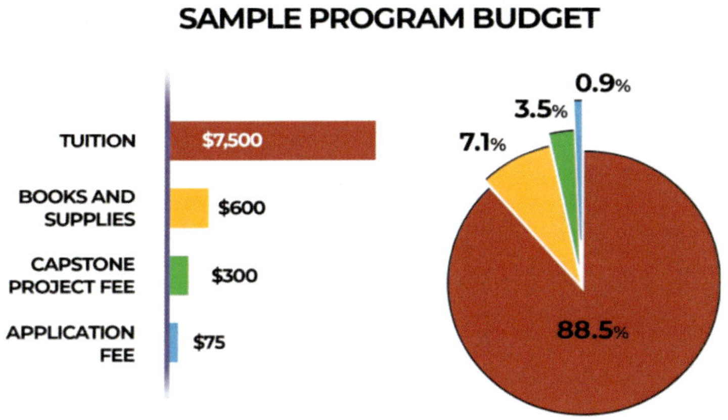

SAMPLE PROGRAM BUDGET

TUITION	$7,500
BOOKS AND SUPPLIES	$600
CAPSTONE PROJECT FEE	$300
APPLICATION FEE	$75

- 88.5%
- 7.1%
- 3.5%
- 0.9%

Figure 27: A sample budget helps people who are interested in your program understand the financial side of enrollment.

Offering flexible payment options and schedules could be a factor for some prospective students who are on the fence about enrolling. For example, allowing students to pay in installments makes it easier for them to spread out the cost over time without having to pay upfront in full. This shows respect and flexibility for students' needs, which can set the right tone for your incoming class.

The program page should also note whether any financial aid is available. If there are scholarships or grants, state the eligibility requirements and provide instructions about how to apply. Some students may also need help coordinating tuition assistance through their employers.

Measuring Impact

Measuring the impact of executive education programs is crucial for assessing their effectiveness and making data-driven improvements. Methods may include pre- and post-program assessments, alumni surveys, and tracking the career progression of graduates. Collecting a mix of quantitative and qualitative data allows administrators and advisors to assess whether program outcomes were as anticipated.

Additionally, this information may be useful for marketing and advertising to future cohorts. If you know that the majority of program alumni negotiate for higher salaries or promotions, you can use that data as tangible evidence of the program's value. Your university may also benefit from analyzing the findings of third-party research entities like Gallup.

Unlike purely internal surveys, Gallup solicits feedback from alumni of multiple institutions to compile in national reports like the 2018 Strada-Gallup Alumni Survey: Mentoring College Students to Success. This survey sought to determine how students' careers and well-being were impacted by mentoring relationships in college.

The general Gallup Alumni Survey quantifies how engaged alumni are at work, evaluates alumni well-being, and measures how alumni feel about their alma maters after graduation. Some schools like The Busch School of Business at The Catholic University of America even hire Gallup to compare their programs to national averages.

Although the Gallup Alumni Survey is targeted toward undergraduate education, there are still potential learnings for programs at any level of academia. It's also important to note that research on executive education programs may be rare compared to studies with a broader scope.

Financial Stability and Resource Management

Understanding the financial needs of your executive education program is essential to protecting its longevity. As an advisory board member, you can take a more targeted view of the program's financial state than general university staff who may need to account for multiple programs within a department. A comprehensive analysis of the program should be driven by concrete financial objectives rather than vague goals like "year-over-year growth."

By conducting a thorough assessment of projected costs, revenue, and return on investment, you and your peers can determine the exact financial outcomes required to sustain the program over time. These metrics will serve as the foundation for allocating resources and financial planning on an ongoing basis.

Figure 28: Expenses may relate to multiple different functional areas such as marketing and software.

It's important, however, to remember that startup expenses to launch the new program are likely to skew the numbers in the first years the program is offered. For example, the university will need to recruit all faculty, advisors, and other personnel to support the program. These costs to build an initial roster of personnel will be much higher than ongoing recruitment expenses to expand the program or address routine attrition.

In addition to startup expenses, your budget projections should account for periodic upgrades and improvements. The equipment and digital platforms you use to launch your program won't last indefinitely. Items like projectors and lab computers will eventually degrade, and digital tools will become outdated. Plus, incorporating the latest technologies and learning management systems can be a selling point to prospective applicants.

You should also consider investing in the personal development of your faculty. Instructors are critically important to the success of your program. The participation of well-known experts can draw in applicants and distinguish your executive education program from competitors. Funding professional development opportunities like industry conferences ensures instructors are up to date on emerging trends and maintains their personal connections within their fields.

Furthermore, some of your expenses and costs may vary based on other conditions. If you have a long waitlist of applicants who are interested in your executive education programs, then you can likely scale back on your marketing and promotion for the next few sessions. Those funds could then be used to add courses or expand the program in response to such existing high demand.

After each change in your budget, compare your current progress to projections to see whether there are any discrepancies. Some performance metrics will be ongoing, while others might focus on a specific initiative or subset of the program. Input from students and instructors about their experiences with the program may also help you identify concerns that aren't easily captured by quantitative metrics.

Diversifying Revenue Streams

In general, universities and other academic institutions have multiple revenue streams outside of tuition. Relying solely on tuition is risky since fluctuations in enrollment can significantly affect the amount earned from that single source. If enrollment for a given period is low, raising costs or outright canceling courses could alienate students who are already committed to your program.

Fortunately, there are many alternative sources of revenue such as corporate donations, alumni gifts, and investments. Earnings from campus food services and the bookstore tend to be minimal but shouldn't be overlooked. Your institution may also be eligible for federal grants and state-level funding that can be used to supplement tuition and fees.

POTENTIAL SOURCES OF REVENUE

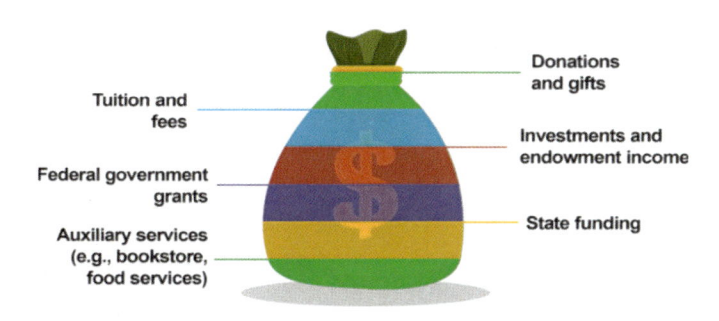

- Tuition and fees
- Federal government grants
- Auxiliary services (e.g., bookstore, food services)
- Donations and gifts
- Investments and endowment income
- State funding

Figure 29: Exploring several revenue streams ensures your program isn't wholly reliant on any single source.

While your program should seek to have diversified revenue streams even during periods of stability, having multiple sources of income insulates your program against economic downturns, natural disasters, or other threats to continuity. This was highly evident during the start of the pandemic when schools were suddenly faced with the need to close. Over a span of mere weeks, more than 1,100 colleges and universities throughout the country ceased in-person operations.

Maintaining multiple revenue streams makes it easier to react in a crisis situation, pay for unexpected expenses, or recover from sudden changes in enrollment. By actively seeking external funding, your executive education programs can create new revenue streams and alleviate dependence on tuition fees.

Emphasize Program Benefits

Effective fundraising strategies require a clear understanding of the program's mission, value proposition, and impact on alumni. Being able to articulate your program's value is essential when seeking financial support from alumni or corporate sponsors. Highlighting success stories and your program's contributions to the industry can attract potential donors and clarify how funds will be spent to benefit projects of public importance.

For instance, at Stanford Human-Centered Artificial Intelligence (HAI), executive education courses focus on emerging issues related to advanced technologies. Students learn about the safe, ethical use of AI and how to properly implement artificial intelligence into their respective organizations. These program elements could bolster fundraising efforts by highlighting how Stanford HAI courses contribute to corporate responsibility and data security in a broad range of industries.

Engage with Alumni

Alumni networks are a valuable resource for fundraising. Reaching out to program graduates maintains the university's connection with executives long after they've completed their course of study.

Something as simple as a periodic mailing or newsletter can keep these individuals informed about networking opportunities, new educational opportunities, and alumni events.

Alumni who are more engaged and personally invested in the university are more likely to make financial contributions, recommend programs to peers, or respond to surveys about the impact of the program. Since alumni of executive education programs are often prominent figures in their respective organizations, their affiliation with the school can have a profound effect on others. Even if the people they interact with aren't part of the target market for executive education programs, those individuals may still pursue continuing education by taking other courses.

Imagine that the CEO of a mid-sized company completes an executive education program with your university. They hang their certificate on the wall in their office and occasionally wear a jacket with your school's logo on it. They also update their social media profiles and corporate bio to reflect their participation in your program.

Because of these actions, several people notice the CEO's affiliation with your university. The CFO becomes interested in continuing education and gets in touch with the CEO to ask more questions about the program. Simultaneously, an entry-level employee who's considering a master's degree recalls that the CEO endorsed your school and looks up which degrees are available.

If either of these individuals eventually enrolls for even a single course, that revenue can be traced back to alumni influence. Therefore, even if alumni don't make financial contributions, they can still play a part in driving growth by serving as informal representatives for your university.

Explore Grants and Research Opportunities

Most public and private schools are eligible for federal government grants or financial assistance. In 2018, federal investments in higher education totaled $149 billion. The vast majority of federal aid is spent on individual students in the form of scholarships, subsidized loans, or need-based aid like Pell grants.

However, there are still opportunities for institutions themselves to secure federal aid. Of the $149 billion spent in 2018, 27 percent funded research and projects that would benefit the public. Meanwhile, 8 percent of that total went toward federal contracts to pay for government use of labs and research.

Interestingly, state and local contributions generally exceed federal funding. In 2020, state and local governments allocated $321 billion for higher education. Most of the funds were spent on routine operating expenses such as libraries and student services, but 11 percent was earmarked for capital improvements and maintenance.

Sponsorships from companies interested in aligning their brand with the program can also offer significant financial backing. Boeing, for example, has a longstanding collaboration with Caltech to innovate and research new technologies for use in Boeing products. Their relationship dates all the way back to early 1932 when Boeing used Caltech's aeronautics wind tunnel for testing. Their relationship expanded in 2004 when Boeing and Caltech entered a strategic partnership focused on advanced technologies such as thermal ignition hazards and quantum nanophotonics.

Collaborative partnerships and philanthropic giving are on the rise. According to a survey by the Council for Advancement and Support of Education, donations to academic institutions increased by 12.5 percent in 2022, reaching a total of $59.5 billion across all responding schools. Roughly 61 percent of donations were made by organizations, while 16 percent came from unaffiliated individuals who were not graduates of the receiving institution.

Most of the contributions were designated for scholarship funds or research projects. Those types of restricted endowments come with limitations on how they can be used, which allows donors to only support initiatives of their choosing. In 2022, restricted endowments made up almost 80 percent of total donations.

Crowdfunding Platforms

It may sound unorthodox, but many student groups now use crowdfunding platforms as part of their larger fundraising strategies. Crowdfunding can be combined with social media outreach to mobilize support from alumni, industry professionals, and members of the general public with an interest in a particular niche. These student groups are often responsible for funding their own activities, which may include trips, research projects, or sporting events.

Some schools even have designated pages and points of contact to facilitate crowdfunding. The University of New Orleans has a designated website that lists student projects. This provides a centralized location for alumni or other potential donors to evaluate various projects and determine whether they would like to contribute.

During the 2023 year, for instance, the student branch of the Institute of Electrical and Electronics Engineers (IEEE) created a crowdfunding request for $5,000. The funds were earmarked for lab materials, competition fees, IEEE events, and student projects. The university even has a messaging system that encourages prospective donors to text a number and sign up for notifications about the group's progress.

This case highlights how modern technology has affected traditional means of fundraising. By embracing new approaches like crowdfunding, your executive education programs have a better chance of successfully funding projects and initiatives. The exact design of the campaign would need to be adjusted to reflect the level of the program and the target audiences for executive issues, but there's no indication that these differences would inhibit the overall effectiveness of crowdfunding as a practice.

Looking Ahead

This chapter discussed the necessary steps to establish and maintain an executive education program. You learned how to cultivate interest from prospective students, streamline the admissions process, and appeal to executives in a broad variety of industries. Next, you discovered best practices to manage resources and predict operating expenses as your program expands.

Chapter Seven will introduce performance metrics that can be used to measure progress and examine ways to foster a culture of continuous growth within your program. This includes a section about promoting innovative thinking, reacting to change, and approaching emerging technologies with an open mindset.

7

Continuous Improvement and Evaluating Program Success

Evaluating the success of your executive education program is an essential part of driving continuous improvement and adapting to the changing needs of students. Conducting periodic assessments of your progress also encourages transparency, honesty, and a culture that values feedback. When continuous improvement is a core commitment of your organization, it's easier to maintain momentum since stakeholders already recognize the importance of growth, optimization, and data-driven decision-making.

One of the most famous case studies about continuous improvement leads back to the automotive industry. Leading into the 1950s, Toyota was struggling to compete and avoid outright bankruptcy. Company leaders knew that they needed to make a change, and they wisely concentrated their efforts on a combination of culture and production processes. This was the start of the Toyota Production System (TPS).

TPS taught employees that mistakes were learning opportunities and chances to improve upon existing processes. Instead of demanding perfection from an imperfect system, Toyota encouraged employees to identify inefficiencies and make suggestions about how to eliminate waste. The company also introduced the idea of rapid process improvements, or kaizen, which involved making many small adjustments that would accumulate to great effect over time.

The TPS model gave rise to a new mindset about lean production and streamlining workflows to minimize waste, the toll on employees, and process inefficiencies. Lean Six Sigma (LSS) would later emerge as another framework for driving continuous improvement. In particular, LSS focuses on improving quality, increasing uniformity, and creating value for customers.

The main LSS technique, also known as DMAIC, has five key stages: define, measure, analyze, improve, and control. The process begins by defining a problem and measuring data to further characterize necessary improvements. From there, teams analyze the data and make suggestions to improve upon the process. The final stage involves implementing controls to sustain solutions and avoid the same problems in the future.

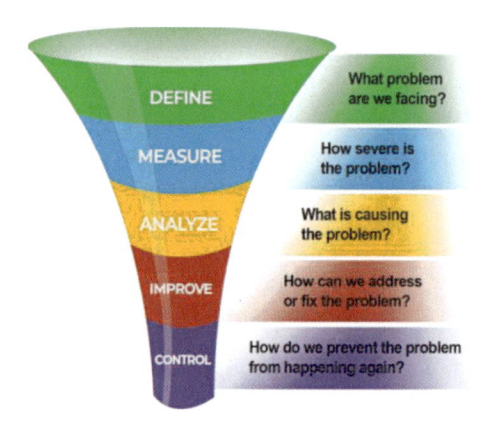

Figure 30: Each stage of DMAIC poses a central question about the problem.

If these types of models don't appeal to you as an advisor, you can always develop your own plan that's tailored to your university or department staff. As you assess the current state of your organization, consider the following best practices:

- Communicate openly about improvements and encourage employees to make suggestions.
- Provide training or workshops to build problem-solving skills among instructors, staff, and other members of your team.
- Allow employees to experiment and take risks as they explore new methods.
- Recognize individuals who contribute ideas or improve upon a process to make it more efficient.

Highlighting the Impact of Continuous Improvement

To reinforce your commitment to continuous improvement, your program can publicly share the actions you've taken to evolve and maintain a growth mindset. The University of Waterloo has an entire section of its website dedicated to continuous improvement. Users can read about the Continuous Improvement and Change Management Community of Practice, scroll through case studies from the university, and access educational resources.

One case study describes recent improvements to the employee handbook for the Office of the Provost. None of the processes for the Office of the Provost were formalized or recorded in a functional manner. The drive was unorganized and potentially contained out-of-date information. These issues made it extremely difficult to continue normal operations if the usual point of contact was out of the office due to illness or other obligations.

The University of Waterloo established a procedure to update the drive and sort documents into a binder that any employee could access in the office or online. Each portion of the binder was assigned a designated owner to manage the materials and update the hard copy and digital version as needed. Routine processes were broken down to include step-by-step instructions. These actions minimized the likelihood of disruption from employee absences and reduced clutter from disorganized documents.

The continuous improvement case study on the University of Waterloo website details the actions the team took, how they identified the problem, and the results of their efforts. Another section describes the positive outcomes in greater detail and notes the challenges the department faced while completing this project. Having this information clearly available makes it easier to identify learnings and understand how the group tackled issues like sticking to the schedule.

Program Evaluations

There are many different philosophies about how to evaluate the success of educational programs. These assessments confirm that the program is delivering the intended results and staying in alignment with its original overarching goals. They can also be utilized to gain support for the program by providing tangible data to present to stakeholders such as prospective applicants, instructors, advisory board members, or corporate partners.

By presenting concrete data and testimonials about the success of the program, your institution can show the expected return on investment and demonstrate the value to students. An effective program evaluation should follow this general process:

1. Define the scope of the evaluation and which questions you hope to answer.
2. Establish the process for conducting the evaluation and identify which models the evaluators will use, if applicable.
3. Complete the evaluation.

4. Analyze the resulting data to identify strengths and weaknesses within the program.
5. Identify strategies to mitigate weaknesses and build upon strengths.
6. Implement changes and communicate your actions to the larger organization.

The Kirkpatrick Model

As you develop an implementation plan, your team might decide to use a formal framework like the Kirkpatrick Model to carry out your evaluation. Dr. Donald L. Kirkpatrick invented this method of evaluating training programs in the 1950s, and it would go on to become one of the most widely used models in the world.

LEVELS OF THE KIRKPATRICK MODEL

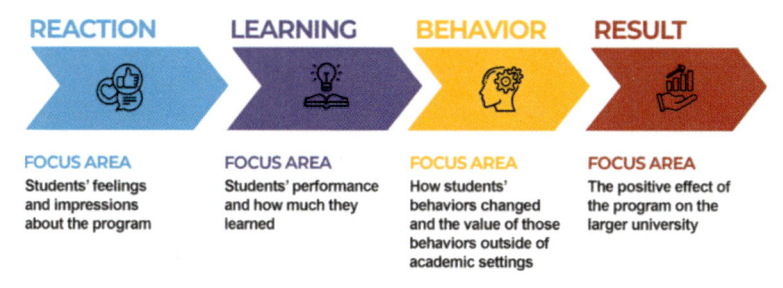

REACTION	LEARNING	BEHAVIOR	RESULT
FOCUS AREA Students' feelings and impressions about the program	**FOCUS AREA** Students' performance and how much they learned	**FOCUS AREA** How students' behaviors changed and the value of those behaviors outside of academic settings	**FOCUS AREA** The positive effect of the program on the larger university

Figure 31: This method of evaluation considers multiple facets of how students experience the program and relate to the university as a whole.

The Kirkpatrick Model breaks each program down into four separate areas: reaction, learning, behavior, and results. Each part has its own metrics and indicators, and not all stages will apply with equal weight depending on the scope of the assessment. A single course, for instance, is more likely to be evaluated based on what students have learned, while an entire program could be assessed with the full model to measure qualities like organizational impact.

Your program doesn't necessarily need to use an established method like the Kirkpatrick model, but these frameworks provide an alternative way to approach the question of performance, impact, and adherence to design. You might uncover more areas for improvement using multiple methodologies than by using the same approach every time.

External Evaluators

Your university may benefit from hiring third-party evaluators, especially if internal metrics indicate the program is adhering to its original design and performing well. Generally, academic consulting firms are able to assess the overall program or examine a specific area of performance. Working with an external party adds more objectivity to your findings and includes the perspectives of individuals who aren't intimately familiar with your organization.

For example, Gray Associates is a Massachusetts-based firm that specializes in higher education. The firm uses its own Program Evaluation System (PES) to evaluate academic programs. The PES uses software and comparative data analytics to assess each program in the context of the larger industry. Its dashboard also provides information about DE&I, student performance, and program economics.

Program Impact on Participants and Organizations

Executive education programs can play a pivotal role in enhancing the knowledge, skills, and capabilities of professionals in leadership positions. When properly designed and implemented, these programs profoundly influence participating executives who later apply learnings and takeaways within their respective organizations.

Evaluating the personal impact of your program confirms whether it's providing value and having the desired effect on students. This is an entirely separate process from program evaluations that determine whether a program adheres to its original design. As such, you and other advisors may need to collaborate on multiple types of assessments.

The impact of your executive education program should be measured with a combination of quantitative and qualitative methods to maintain a holistic view. Quantitative data encourages a more objective perspective and includes measurable metrics such as ratings and completion percentages. Qualitative data, on the other hand, captures the emotional side of the student experience by analyzing open-ended feedback like testimonials.

QUANTITATIVE DATA
- Numerical ratings
- Completion percentages
- Number of student complaints

QUALITATIVE DATA
- Testimonials
- Success stories
- Long-form reviews
- Interview responses

Figure 32: Using multiple sources of quantitative and qualitative data allows you to develop a more thorough understanding of the program.

Quantitative data can be easier to track and trend since qualitative data is inherently less structured. Two open-ended responses on a feedback sheet could address drastically different areas of the program. However, it is sometimes possible to convert qualitative data into general quantifiable terms. For example, you could determine whether written reviews are negative or positive and monitor the resulting percentages over time.

Needs Assessments and Student Satisfaction

Referring to the needs assessment from the initial design phases of the program can simplify the process of evaluating whether those needs have been met according to student feedback. The assessment should identify which skills students will acquire and the expected outcomes for how the program will improve their personal readiness to lead. This information will help you recognize whether your program is fulfilling its commitments.

If your university's executive education program is still relatively new, this is also an opportunity to ensure that the needs assessment matches how students perceive their needs. If there's a disconnect between those perspectives, students may be unsatisfied because they have a different understanding of their collective knowledge gaps and priorities.

When you assess student satisfaction, be clear about the purpose of the survey, questionnaire, or interview. Otherwise, you may receive unclear feedback that's irrelevant to the topic you're currently investigating. If you only ask for students' opinions in a general sense, you might receive negative survey responses about individual faculty members or the faulty air conditioning in a particular classroom when you really wanted to know how students felt about the impact of the program's content.

Program Goals and Learning Objectives

Another critical aspect of evaluating impact is whether students feel that program goals and learning objectives were met. These goals are typically centered on building leadership capabilities, enhancing decision-making skills, driving innovation, and managing strategic change. For industry-specific programs, competencies may also relate to core responsibilities of leading an organization in that field.

Pre- and post-program evaluations provide insight into students' capabilities before and after completing the program. Collecting this data adds another layer of nuance that could prove valuable later. Imagine that a student rates their problem-solving skills as 1 of 5 on the pre-enrollment survey, indicating they struggle with this aspect of leadership. If they rate their problem-solving skills as 2 of 5 after completing the program, that's an improvement. However, if you didn't know they started at the lowest level, it might look like the program wasn't effective at improving their abilities in that area.

It's also important to consider the role of time. It may take several months for alumni to use their new skills enough to properly reflect on the program. Follow-up assessments and surveys can provide multiple opportunities for graduates to engage after they've had sufficient time to apply learnings in their current positions. Additionally, executives may not be able to practice some skills, such as managing a major change initiative, until the opportunity presents itself.

Efficiency and Wasted Effort

Your impact evaluation should also analyze outcomes in terms of efficiency and relevance. Students may have feedback about whether the program utilizes resources in an efficient way and minimizes wasted effort. If you detect a problem, trace the negative outcome back to its underlying cause whenever possible. Not only does this identify the cause of the issue, but it also allows you to investigate whether the problem is systemic throughout the entire program.

For example, imagine that students report feeling frustrated about missing documents and assignment materials on the online platform after completing the first course in the program. The negative comments come from different faculty members and courses, so you don't believe it's a knowledge gap involving a single individual.

When your team delves into the issue, you realize many instructors don't know how to upload documents in bulk. Instead, they've been individually attaching each file by hand. The resulting process is time consuming and frustrating, and it also increases the likelihood of mistakes like accidentally overlooking a document.

As a result of student feedback, the department writes an instruction sheet with screenshots to help instructors understand the more efficient method. They make the change and the problem isn't repeated in subsequent courses. Students see that their feedback is valued, which further encourages them to submit their thoughts in the future.

Relevance of Program Topics

Your program evaluation should also examine the relevance of course content on an ongoing basis. You may notice there's more or less demand for a particular topic as students' needs change or they arrive with different levels of competency than previous cohorts. Some courses will have a naturally shorter functional life than others if they're focused on rapidly changing topics like cutting-edge technologies.

Creating a skills matrix is one technique you can use to anticipate students' needs, priorities, and interests. This type of matrix lists several skills and displays associated ratings for a group of people based on their relationships with those topics. Ratings are divided by each person's level of expertise and their interest in that skill. Someone with an expertise rating of 5 of 5 might have an interest level of 1 of 5 because they've already invested so much time and energy in honing that particular skill.

Asking students to reflect on their interests and existing knowledge through surveys or assessments ensures that you have direct feedback about their priorities. If you notice low ratings in the interest category from most respondents, then the data might be signaling that your course on that topic is no longer relevant. You can also use a skills matrix to show different competencies and interests among staff or advisory board members.

	Employee 1		Employee 2		Employee 3	
SKILLS	Expertise	Interest	Expertise	Interest	Expertise	Interest
Communication	5	3	5	5	3	5
Diversity	3	1	3	3	1	3
Artificial intelligence	2	3	2	2	3	2
Board governance	4	2	4	4	2	4
Innovation	3	4	3	3	4	3
Change management	2	2	2	2	2	2
Finance and budgeting	4	1	4	4	1	4

Figure 33: A skills matrix simplifies the process of identifying each person's interests and comparing skill sets in a larger group.

A skills matrix is a convenient method of presenting information in an easily digestible format. Stakeholders can quickly draw conclusions from the data, especially if the ratings are color coded. Because of its visual nature, this technique works best with small groups. If your executive education department extremely large or highly diversified into multiple separate programs, a traditional presentation style is more likely to be effective.

Improvement and Innovation

Identifying areas for improvements is an important step toward growth, but developing innovative solutions is just as essential. In addition to addressing existing challenges in academia and business, executive education programs must also keep an eye on future opportunities.

The rapid pace of business and technological expansion presents new avenues for development and innovation. Staying informed about emerging trends, disruptive technologies, and shifting needs in leadership allows your organization to adapt and remain relevant within the crowded market of higher education.

Research by the Association to Advance Collegiate Schools of Business indicates that the pandemic substantially increased the demand for upskilling, reskilling, and flexible instructional methods. Executive education programs invested heavily in remote learning, increasing the use of instructional designers by 70 percent. Schools also incorporated new digital tools and encouraged a more collaborative relationship between course instructors and online instructional design teams.

Between disruptive technologies and a societal shift toward new models of education, organizations that fail to grow will soon lag behind the competition. Executives often enroll in continuing education to update their skills, discover cutting-edge techniques, and refresh the management concepts they learned in the past.

In order to meet these needs, your executive education programs must rapidly adapt and stay ahead of what executives might learn about disruptive trends on their own. For example, a present-day executive education course on bias and machine learning algorithms should look drastically different than a course from 2021. Even though 2021 might seem recent, technology evolves so quickly that years-old revelations about AI capabilities might be common knowledge by now and no longer valuable to students who are leading at the forefront of their industries.

Types of Innovation

Innovation can be split into two major categories: product innovation and business process innovation. The former encompasses both products and services. This system takes into account the difference between innovating external outputs that generate revenue and innovating internally to create new methods of production or systems of operating.

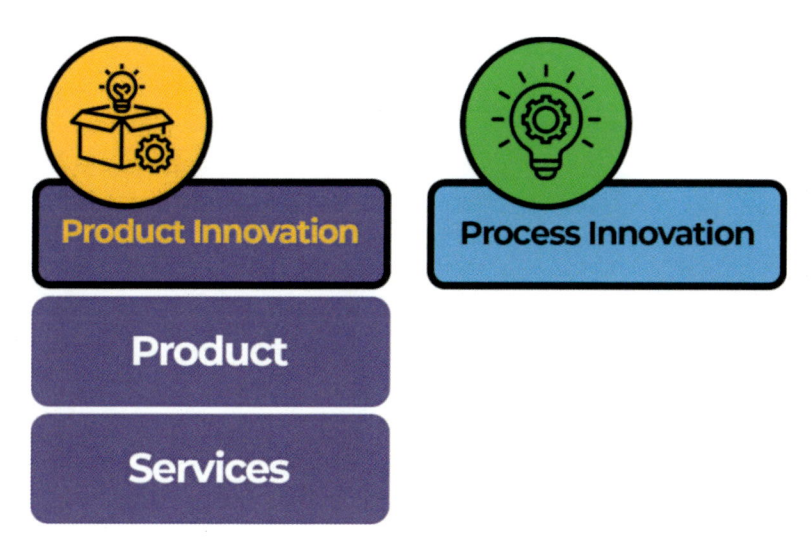

Figure 34: Product innovation and process innovation are distinct from one another with separate core purposes.

Even though leaders overwhelmingly believe innovation is a positive behavior and cultural trend, creating something truly novel is exceptionally difficult. The Annual Business Survey (ABS) conducted by the National Center for Science and Engineering Statistics and the Census Bureau provides some insight by analyzing innovation at U.S. companies. The questions on the ABS are based on the Oslo Manual developed by the Statistical Office of the European Union and the Organisation for Economic Co-operation and Development.

In the 2020 ABS report, only four percent of companies introduced an innovative product that was entirely new to the market during the two-year period from 2017 to 2019. Meanwhile, seven percent of companies unveiled a product that was only new to the business itself, not to the larger industry. This is an important distinction since creating a new version of an existing product or service may still involve innovative thinking, but it's not the same as inventing an entirely new product.

Feeling free to take risks and fail is central to any form of innovation. However, a 2019 study by the professional services company Ernst & Young (EY) shows that perceptions at the executive level may not always translate down through the entire organization. Despite 79 percent of C-suite executives stating their organizations were accepting of failure, only a quarter of entry-level workers agreed.

This discrepancy reinforces the need for transparency and self-awareness in the upper echelons of modern organizations. While the advisory board or the department chair may feel that your university's executive education programs support innovation, your junior faculty and support staff may not feel the same way.

Incorporating Outside Perspectives

Collaborating with external experts, industry leaders, and faculty is an excellent way to infuse your executive education programs with new perspectives and approaches. Hosting guest lecturers and industry partnerships invites diverse viewpoints into your program and provides your existing team with an opportunity to learn from others.

If you invite a guest lecturer or hold a meeting with industry leaders, be open about your receptiveness to feedback. This communicates that you're open to suggestions about how to improve your programs. Otherwise, people who are only tangentially affiliated with your university may not feel comfortable expressing their ideas even if they recognize flaws or outdated content in your programs.

Soliciting outside perspectives also enables you to build a network of subject matter experts for future collaboration. Harvard Business School and the University's of Pennsylvania's Wharton School of Business are notable examples of academic institutions that have used external partnerships and innovation to their advantage. Harvard introduced the Business Analytics Program after working with subject matter experts from industry. Similarly, Wharton responded to the demand for AI by establishing an online AI for Business program.

These initiatives showcase how two of the most prominent academic institutions are continuously assessing the needs of students, seeking out experts, and enhancing their programs with the latest knowledge about developing topics. However, these schools also have access to a wealth of resources and substantial endowments that enable them to take more risk than universities with limited budgets for improvements.

Communicating Value

Gaining support for innovative opportunities is crucial to the success of your program, but you may encounter resistance from decision-makers about the allocation of resources. Stakeholder engagement can help you garner support by showing key individuals how funds are being used to improve the program and provide a better experience to students.

In EY's 2019 study, 42 percent of executives cited lack of funding as a significant barrier to innovation. When possible, highlight how innovations align with organizational goals and contribute to the reputation of the school as a whole. This fosters a more collaborative mindset where departments and programs share resources instead of competing over them.

Furthermore, advocating for additional funding is likely to be easier if your organization has designated individuals who are responsible for driving innovation. The EY survey revealed that although 90 percent of executives report board involvement in innovation, the senior leadership team has the most impact on innovation. Therefore, even if you aren't a top officer of your organization or university, you still have the ability to effect change as a leader and advisor.

If you're struggling to convince key stakeholders about the promise of a new initiative, consider a pilot program or a targeted project on a smaller scale. These programs consume fewer resources and have less inherent risk than a fully funded initiative. A pilot program allows you to test ideas, gather feedback, and make adjustments before attempting a full implementation of your plan.

If you can demonstrate positive outcomes on a smaller scale, you can use those results as leverage in future negotiations with stakeholders. Seeing tangible evidence of success can help sway supporters to your side and show that you're committed to a data-driven approach to innovation.

Looking Ahead

In this chapter, we discussed the need for continuous improvement and how to foster an organizational culture that values growth. You learned how to conduct program and impact evaluations and discovered different techniques to analyze challenges moving forward. Lastly, you considered various strategies to promote innovation, gain support from stakeholders, and secure resources for new program initiatives.

The final chapter of this book will explore how to balance your roles as an executive, leader, and advisory board member. This will include a dialogue about how to manage conflicts of interests and balance competing obligations between multiple organizations.

8

Balancing Multiple Leadership Roles

Working professionals who are simultaneously serving as leaders and advisory board members must maintain a delicate balance between each commitment. Time management, communication skills, and self-awareness are essential to succeed in both capacities. Otherwise, taking on multiple leadership positions can become overwhelming or lead to burnout.

If you choose to accept a second role, it's critical to have the right mindset. Your professional responsibilities and the demands of the advisory board can complement one another rather than turning into competing priorities. The observations you make as a leader can inform your recommendations as an advisor, while the input you gain from your fellow board members can help you develop a new perspective on challenges in the workplace.

RESPONSIBILITIES OF MULTIPLE ROLES

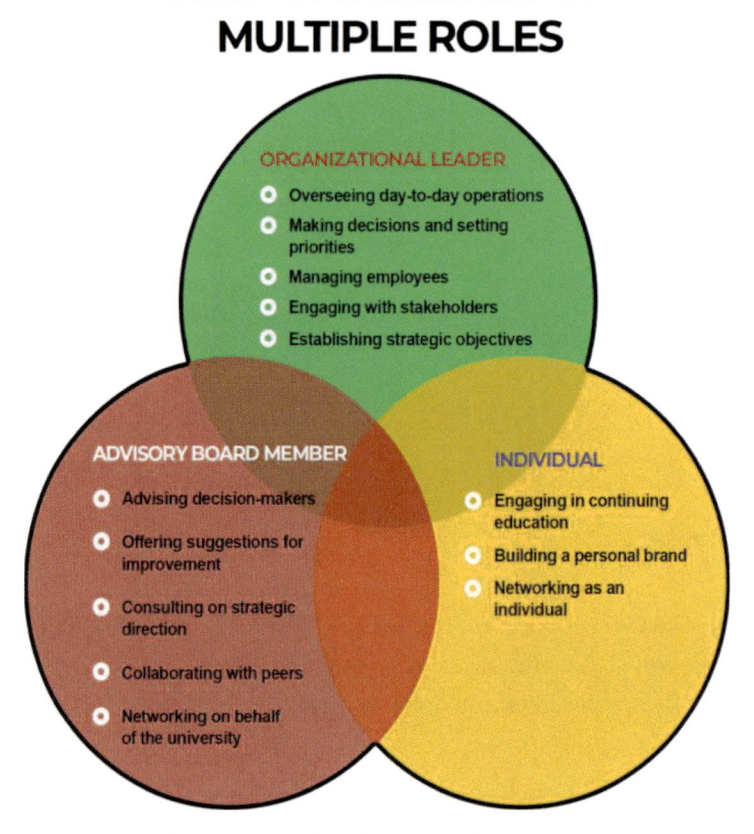

ORGANIZATIONAL LEADER
- Overseeing day-to-day operations
- Making decisions and setting priorities
- Managing employees
- Engaging with stakeholders
- Establishing strategic objectives

ADVISORY BOARD MEMBER
- Advising decision-makers
- Offering suggestions for improvement
- Consulting on strategic direction
- Collaborating with peers
- Networking on behalf of the university

INDIVIDUAL
- Engaging in continuing education
- Building a personal brand
- Networking as an individual

Figure 35: Advisory board members must balance their responsibility to the university against their individual priorities and the demands of their organizations.

Your position as a leader demands active involvement and management. An advisory role is less involved and focuses on providing guidance and direction. While some of these elements will inevitably overlap, understanding the unique nature of each role will make it easier for you to navigate conflicts and create a mutually beneficial relationship between your obligations.

Time Management and Prioritization

Regardless of your exact responsibilities, there will always be demands on your time and attention. When you're filling multiple roles, it's even more critical to prioritize tasks, set realistic goals, and communicate your own limitations to others on your team. If you don't take clear steps to protect your time, you may end up neglecting one area or making mistakes from attempting too many tasks at once.

Prioritize and Delegate

As you assess your commitments, identify the most critical tasks and prioritize them in terms of their impact and urgency. Consider the consequences if you don't personally handle a certain obligation such as attending a meeting or compiling a report. There are some responsibilities that only you can address; less pressing tasks can probably be delegated.

After deciding that you can delegate a task, collaborate with other colleagues and members of your team to share the workload. In some cases, another person within your organization may be eager to assist you, and you can simply provide feedback on the final product. If a junior employee completed most of the task, turn it into a mentoring opportunity and recognize that individual. If it's a peer, you can offer to reciprocate and repay the favor in the future when they're struggling.

There's no shortage of techniques to manage your priorities but it might take some experimentation before you find which ones are worth adding to your personal toolbox. Ranking tasks in a physical planner is helpful for some people, while others use digital productivity tools to keep track of their schedules. You might even benefit from completing a prioritization exercise like making an Eisenhower Matrix.

As its name suggests, the Eisenhower Matrix was invented by Dwight D. Eisenhower, a former U.S. president and the Allied Supreme Commander during WWII. He invented his own method of establishing priorities in these high-profile, high-stakes positions by analyzing the relationship between importance and urgency.

It's easy to accidentally conflate these two ideas, but important tasks don't automatically need to be completed immediately. Similarly, you might encounter urgent, time-sensitive tasks that aren't that important compared to other priorities. The Eisenhower Matrix puts these two factors on opposite sides of a square.

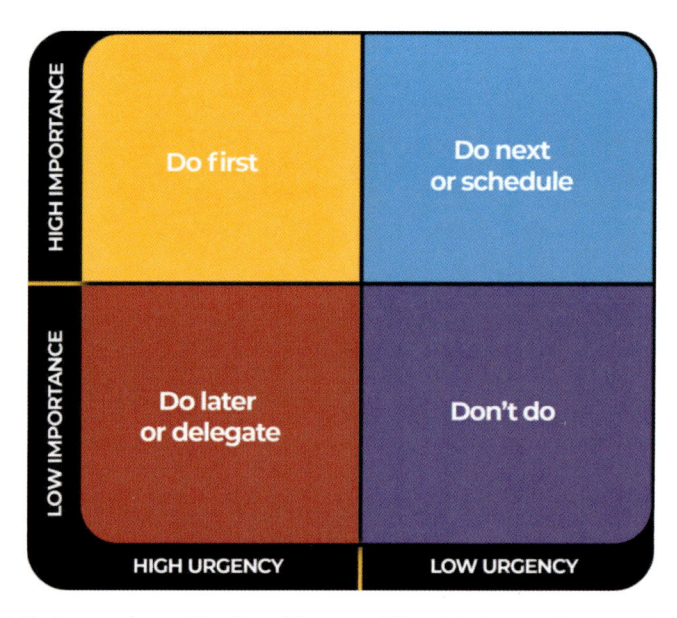

Figure 36: Tasks mapped on an Eisenhower Matrix can fall into one of four quadrants based on urgency and importance.

If you know something is urgent and important, you should personally complete it as soon as possible. When that task is finished, move on to important tasks that aren't as urgent. As you progress to responsibilities that have low importance, ask yourself whether they truly need your personal attention. If you deem that an obligation of low importance is still urgent, delegate it to someone else. A task that's low urgency and low importance most likely doesn't need any action at all.

However, as you consider your matrix, bear in mind that tasks assigned to one category won't always stay in the same quadrant. A task with low urgency and low importance might not need to be addressed in the present, but as its completion date draws nearer, it might become more urgent. This would move it to another quadrant altogether.

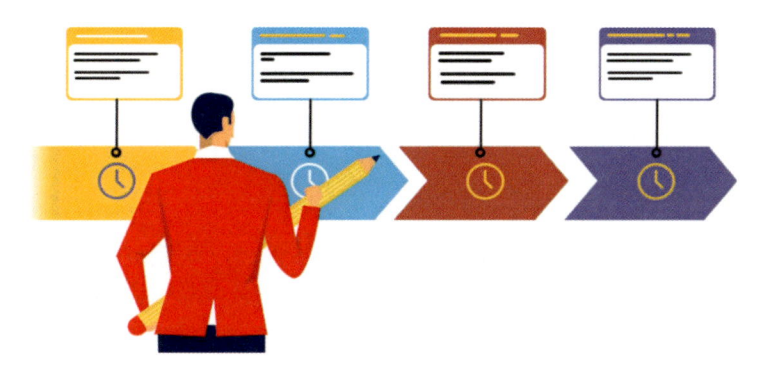

Figure 37: For better visual organization, you can color code tasks in a planner or app to match the Eisenhower Matrix.

Make sure you periodically reevaluate your prioritization of tasks and make adjustments. You'll most likely need to update your to-do list on a daily basis to reflect new additions and tasks you complete throughout the day. This can seem time consuming on its own, which is why many people use productivity tools like Todoist.

Set Boundaries Between Roles

Setting boundaries between roles as a leader of your organization and a university advisory board member makes it simpler to avoid overlapping or conflicting obligations. For example, you could allocate a specific time each day to review any board action items or pressing concerns. Leaving a space for board matters ensures you won't be too stressed or need to cancel another obligation if something urgent suddenly arises.

Clearly defining your purpose also reduces the probability of scope creep, especially if you're a board member at a school that's understaffed in critical leadership positions. In the absence of strong leadership from within administration, faculty or other personnel may turn to the advisory board with matters that are best left with decision-makers. Remember that advisory board members are meant to guide the organization, not invest themselves in managing operational activities.

Maintain Open Communication

Openly communicating with stakeholders and the people in your life ensures everyone around you is informed about your capabilities. When you tell your colleagues, peers, and loved ones about your commitments, it's not as challenging to manage a complex schedule because you're openly exchanging information about each other's priorities.

For example, if you tell other members of the leadership team that you'll need two days off per month to attend advisory board meetings, then they know to anticipate those dates in the future. They might also have travel days or out-of-office meetings they attend on a routine basis. You can even maintain a shared calendar that notes when each person on the leadership team will be unavailable. This way, you can ensure coverage for core responsibilities and work around each other's schedules.

As you communicate your needs, don't forget to prioritize self-care and a healthy work-life balance. Your personal wellness influences your effectiveness in both roles, so burning yourself out with too much work and not enough rest won't be productive in the long run. If you're unable to manage all your obligations, consider requesting additional support such as an assistant to help you delegate and reassign tasks.

Conflicts of Interest

Simultaneously filling multiple roles creates more challenges than just time management. You also need to be mindful of potential conflicts of interest that could arise from having affiliations with more than one organization. Because of this, leaders and decision-makers who are privy to insider knowledge must carefully examine their financial interests and personal connections before accepting new roles.

Figure 38: There are many different conflicts of interest that can stem from personal or professional connections.

Conflicts of interests occur when your personal or professional interests interfere with your ability to make unbiased decisions. Organizations often have their own specific protocols for managing these situations. They may seek out independent third parties if the board and senior leadership team are too directly involved in a particular issue.

In some instances, conflicts of interest are simply unethical or immoral. Serious violations may even run afoul of legal or regulatory rules. For example, Feng Tao, a former professor from the University of Kansas, was convicted of a felony in early 2023 for failing to disclose conflicts of interest. Tao didn't obtain approval for external consulting with the Changjiang Scholar program, which is connected to the Chinese government. Not only did this violate university policy, but it also ran afoul of laws governing federal grants.

When possible, the best solution is simply to avoid situations where conflicts of interest could compromise the integrity of your advice or decisions. For example, an advisory board member who serves as an expert on artificial intelligence might need to recuse themselves if the board is asked to consider proposals from their company during a search for new AI tools.

If you refrain from participating in discussions or decisions that directly affect your own interests, then you're more likely to retain an objective point of view. This helps promote transparency and foster trust in the decision-making process. When conflicts of interest are unavoidable, it's crucial to prominently declare them and acknowledge the potential for unintentional bias. By providing this information, stakeholders will know to assess the situation through the lens of your disclosed relationship to the topic at hand.

Being an Effective and Inspiring Board Member

Reaching the end of this book is just one step on your journey to becoming an informed, empathetic leader. In order to make a lasting impact within your organizations, it's essential to embrace your strengths and acknowledge your weaknesses. Maintaining a growth mindset will enable you to cultivate new opportunities, invest in yourself, and work collaboratively with others to achieve joint goals.

An effective leader understands that their primary objective is to drive results, but it's up to you to chart the path along the way. During your time as an advisory board member, you'll participate in strategic discussions, advise decision-makers, and shape the future of executive education programs as a whole.

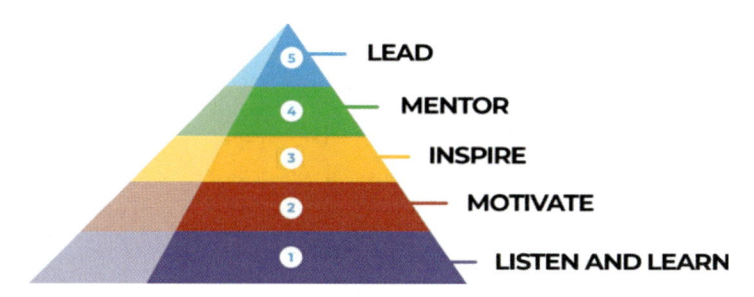

Figure 39: As you become more comfortable, you'll progressively take a more active role to inspire, mentor, and lead others.

As you fulfill your duties, keep an open mind and don't hesitate to challenge your own assumptions about the world around you. Faculty, students, and other stakeholders will look to you for guidance and mentorship. As people in positions of authority, you and your fellow board members must take responsibility for your decisions and uphold ethical standards. Not only does this promote transparency, but it also fosters interpersonal trust that's critical to building ties within the organization.

However, even though serving on an advisory board is an important role, it's also vital for you to protect your time and energy. You can't tackle every task alone, especially if you're simultaneously leading another company or organization. Recognizing that you can't do everything alone allows you to adopt a healthier mindset and delegate tasks as needed. This frees up more time for you to focus on strategic matters and operational responsibilities of high importance.

When possible, make time in your schedule to engage in professional development and update your understanding of industry trends. By taking advantage of training programs and attending conferences, you can broaden your perspectives and discover more about emerging practices or disruptive technologies. The pace of modern innovation isn't showing any signs of slowing, so embrace opportunities to learn and adapt as your career progresses.

Lastly, you shouldn't shy away from chances to innovate on your own. Your imagination can inspire change and expand the possibilities of your university's current programs. By questioning conventional practices and supporting transformational experiences, you can lead your organization into a new era of executive education.

Made in the USA
Columbia, SC
29 November 2023

fdb8a16a-476f-4675-8962-f713574ad9b7R01